VIETNAM '68
Jack's Journal

VIETNAM '68
Jack's Journal

by
Jack W. Jaunal

© 1981, Jack W. Jaunal

Library of Congress Cataloging-in-Publication Data

Jaunal, Jack W. (Jack William), 1927-
    Vietnam '68 : Jack's Journal / by Jack W. Jaunal.

      p. cm.

      ISBN 0-9614188-3-4 : $16.95. — ISBN 0-9614188-4-2 (pbk.) : $9.95
      1. Vietnamese Conflict, 1961-1975—Personal narratives, American.
2. Jaunal, Jack W. (Jack William), 1927-   . I. Title.
DS559.5.J38 1989
959.704'38—dc 19   88-38790
                                                                   CIP

First printing.

The author and the publisher are grateful to all who contributed to making this book
possible. Acknowledgments are made to specific persons and sources throughout the
book. Some of the material is in public domain. The author and publisher have made a
conscientious effort to obtain required permissions. Comments and suggestions,
courteously rendered to the publisher, will be acknowledged and referred to the author.

Printed in United States of America

Publications Consultant: *Lottie Blanton Applewhite*
Production Coordinator: *Peg S. Cheirrett*
Illustrator: *Steve J. Walker*

San Francisco, California

Wasser Communications, Seattle, Washington
Distributor

*Dedicated to my wife
Elizabeth Jaunal,
a two-war veteran
of the three in which I served*

Foreword

Jaunal's Journal is unique in at least two aspects. First, the author records the day-to-day activities of two highly effective American support units – the Third Amphibian Tractor Battalion and the First Reconnaissance Battalion. Both units supported the First Marine Division operations in the Da Nang area during 1968. Second, Jack Jaunal belongs to a group of professionals referred to as "the backbone of the Corps," the Staff Noncommissioned Officer (Staff NCO). As such, his entries reflect the status and stature of the Staff NCO.

The more senior jobs within this group of old "soldiers of the sea" are the First Sergeant and Sergeant Major. There is no civilian equivalent for either position. An incumbent can perhaps best be described as one who is in charge of everything within sight or hearing but who (except in the eyes of his peers and in his own conscience) is ultimately responsible for nothing.

Readers who fought in Vietnam will once again feel the repressive heat and the bone-chilling monsoon rains. They will relive those moments of terror, triumph, and exhilaration. They will recall, with wonder, those incidents of uncommon valor in their ranks and the common, caring, and fatherly leadership practiced by senior NCOs.

From the author's uncluttered straightforward style one can gain an improved insight into the complexities and difficulties of carrying out successful counterinsurgency operations. Where, if he smiles and waves, he may be friendly; if he shoots, assume he's enemy!

Clinton A. Puckett
Sergeant Major, US Marine Corps (Retired)
Sergeant Major of the Marine Corps, 1973-75

August 1988

Preface

Like many veterans of various wars, I remember more than once saying, "I could write a book about this." The two times probably we say it most emphatically are during recruit training and during a wartime experience.

I never wrote anything about my experiences in World War II – all that remains are some memories and a few letters I wrote to my mother.

I never wrote anything about my experiences in Korea – all that remains are more memories and several letters I wrote to my wife.

I did write stories about my experiences in Vietnam. These are compiled now as *VIETNAM '68: Jack's Journal*. This book is a daily record of events, my experiences and thoughts at that time. The stories are true, written at the time recorded or very soon after from notes on a desk calendar, in a pocket notebook, on backs of envelopes, or the top of a C-ration box.

Most of the stories are about the enlisted Marines of "Heat and Steam," Third Amphibian Tractor Battalion and the First Reconnaissance Battalion. The stories are not of the "blood-and-gut" type, or glory, or an exposé – those are for others to write.

Jack W. Jaunal
Sergeant Major, US Marine Corps (Retired)

May 1981

Acknowledgments

My appreciation to the *Seattle Times*, for permission to reprint "Da Nang Battle Began as a Sneak Attack," by Ernie Zaugg; the *Highline Times* to reprint "From Where I'm Standing," by Ginny Anderson; and the Marine Corps Association to reprint "One large success in a lost war," from the November 1978 *Marine Corps GAZETTE*.

12 December 1967

The place is Staging Battalion, Marine Corps Base, Camp Pendleton, California. Most of them are in their teens – Privates, Privates First Class, and Lance Corporals. Among them are the Corporals and Sergeants, not much older, breaking into their twenties. They come in all shapes and sizes, all hours of the day. Most of them are young, the new breed of Marines, on their way to Vietnam.

Sprinkled among this group are the "old salts," Marines with many years of service on their record books. Many are veterans of our last war, Korea. For them this will be their second war. For a few, like me, it is war number three.

For the officers and senior noncommissioned officers, there is a three-day training cycle. A few will be assigned to form a company, from 170 to 200 young Marines, and take them through a nine-day training cycle.

When a Marine arrives at Staging Battalion, he stays in Receiving Company about one day. It does not matter when he reports in – he drops his seabag outside and reports to the check-in building. At the entrance is a Japanese-style gateway of light construction (Torii) with a sign, "Staging Battalion – Gateway to the Pacific."

When the Marine checks in, the duty section will find his card and his Service Record Book (SRB), which should have preceded him. Three punch cards are made, an embossed identification (ID) plate is made, and he is added to the roster. For 800 Marines to check in at one time, usually at night, is not uncommon. And they have problems:

"My seabag was lost at the airport."

"Lost my orders, Sergeant."

"Don't have any money, Sir."

"It was stolen."

"It was lost."

"Where's the chow hall?"

The following day the Marines start to process for shipment. The system is much better than it was during Korea or World War II.

There are ten stations for the Marine to go through at the Administration Building when he begins processing. Station One is to check his Geneva Convention Card. If he does not have one, one is typed for him right there.

Station Two is the start of his record book check. "No record book? Go to Station Eight." At Station Eight a temporary record book is made up, especially the emergency data page. No Marine goes through processing without one. This is the page for next of kin to be notified in case of illness, wounds, or death.

Back to Station Two, check information and orders for correctness. And so it goes. When the Marine arrives at Station Seven he gets an assignment.

"First Marine Division."

"Third Marine Division."

Or some other unit. A few go to Okinawa and Japan, but most are going to Vietnam. Pay records are checked, shots given, allotments made out, and on it goes – the green machine. Upon completion of processing, the Marine checks into the assigned company. In my case, Unit 2000, Second Replacement Company. As I checked in and filled out some forms, the young Corporal noticed my Seattle address.

"You from Seattle, Sarge?"

"Burien."

"Me too!"

The Marine was Corporal Elfeson (Boulevard Park) who had enlisted at the Burien Recruiting Office over a year ago. He was learning the office business after serving a year in Vietnam as a rifleman where he was awarded his Purple Heart.

During his training cycle in the Company, the Marine replacement spends three days in administration matters and then moves to a field training area for nine days. Here he is given classes on Viet Cong mines and booby traps, search of a Viet Cong village, booby-trapped trails, and fires the various weapons available to him, especially the M-16* rifle. A lot has been said about the M-16 – most of it is good. After firing it, I feel it is a good weapon, but must be kept clean to function properly.

An entire Vietnamese village has been built at the Staging Battalion. After a demonstration on the techniques of village search, each Marine applies the lessons learned by going through the village under simulated conditions. The same applies to the Viet Cong trail, to see if he notices mines and booby traps.

Upon completion of the training cycle, Marines are sent to one of three bases to fly out – Travis Air Force Base, Norton Air Force Base, or the Marine Corps Air Station at El Toro.

Telephone calls are made, letters written. Then, to Okinawa aboard a 707. Excess uniforms and gear are stored at Okinawa. After a twenty-four to forty-eight hour stop, those going to Vietnam land at Da Nang.

For me, another tour has started.

*See Glossary

3

23 December 1967

The new breed goes jet-set. That could be the slogan of the new breed Marine.

I can remember the last time going to war, Korea, 1950, and being down in the hold of a crowded troop ship with the sleeping racks stacked six or more high. Seasickness was the order of the day; it took hours to feed, and the trip lasted two weeks.

Now, we travel aboard a World Airlines Boeing 707 charter flight at Travis Air Force Base, California. Thirty minutes after we are airborne the stewardess starts to serve breakfast. At one o'clock in the morning! Four very attractive stewardesses take care of our needs, plenty of room, and in ten hours we land in Japan. Jet, the only way to go!

After a short stop in Japan, the flight continues to Okinawa, our destination before going "south" to Vietnam.

Marines going to and from Vietnam go through Camp Smedley D. Butler in Okinawa for further processing. Final shots, orders and assignments to a flight.

It is Christmas Eve and those going home are trying to get out. Some will not make it in time for Christmas at home. Army buses bring them in at all hours of the day and night. Many of them are still dirty from only a few hours out of Vietnam. Outside, a group of young Marines in their fresh greens, three or four (or more) ribbons on their chests, are smiling and joking, waiting to shove off for home. Passing them are another group, seabags on their shoulders, going to the barracks. These Marines are their replacements going south when their flight is ready. As a couple pass me, I hear one say, "I sure hope I come back," as he looks at the group going home.

His buddy replies, "Don't worry, you'll come back – one way or another, you'll come back."

"Thanks."

As for those of us who are old salts, the senior NCOs on the way south, we would like to be "in country" for Christmas. Since we cannot be home for this one, we can relieve someone who could. We have been at Camp Butler three days and it looks as if not only will I miss Christmas, but the Sergeant I relieve will also miss being home.

"Merry Christmas."

26 December 1967

Building 2732 is the old soldier's home at Camp Smedley D. Butler, the quarters for senior NCOs of the Marine Corps, Master Sergeants and above, going south to Vietnam, or to the States. The average age is probably forty, with twenty years of service behind them. Wars are not new to them, and so there is very little talk of it. Just waiting for a flight out.

One of those waiting for a flight to the States is a robust, heavy-set, ruddy-faced First Sergeant with seven hashmarks (service stripes) on his sleeve. That is at least twenty-eight years as a US Marine. He has been the acting Sergeant Major of the Seventh Marine Regiment. And he looks like a Regimental Sergeant Major (RSM), as the British say, with his snow white hair and a British guardsman's mustache. He is going on a special thirty-day leave in the States and then will serve six more months in Vietnam. Plans to re-enlist over there! When he walks through the camp area, many a young Marine turns to see this old salt go by, and they know he has been to Vietnam by the ribbon on his chest – among the other fourteen or so.

"Say, First," I ask, "Do you know Sergeant Ormsby? He's got Mike Company, Seventh."

"Yeah, he got evacuated out. Don't know if he was hit or got sick. Lot of sickness down there. The water, etc. His outfit took some casualties. Sorry to have to tell you that. Yeah, Ormsby is a good Marine."

When you know them, it always brings the war closer. Ormsby was stationed at the Seattle Recruiting Office, lived on Bainbridge Island. Had a son who was wounded over there about a year ago. The son wanted to go back to Vietnam and his mom was not too crazy about that.

Seems as if some of those extending their tours in Republic of Vietnam (RVN) for six months are aviation Marines. One Sergeant Major of a Marine squadron will have twenty-five months in Vietnam when he completes his next six months. I have not noticed many infantrymen extending their tours. No wonder.

The Third Division Bandmaster is on his way home, enlisted in the Corps in 1942. He is a Master Gunnery Sergeant; he plans to retire next October.

"Not enough bandmasters in the Corps; figure I'll retire before they send me back again."

We talked about Seattle, once he heard me mention it.

"Good town, Seattle," he said, "always treated Marines good there."

"I had the band at El Toro. We came up for a couple of Seafair parades and the Armed Forces Pageant."

A Gunnery Sergeant came over to visit a friend yesterday. The Gunny was going home, his friend was going south. The Gunny was forty-seven years old and had seen his third war.

"Why don't you retire?" his friend asked.

"Would like to make Master Sergeant before I get out. Maybe this time." The Gunny is a metalsmith.

We hear First Sergeants are shot in Vietnam, Sergeants Major also. So here we come. Those of us going south tonight are the old salts. About forty years of age, twenty-plus years in service, and grown children at home. Three Sergeants Major and eight First Sergeants on the way. Look out Vietnam – here we come, the mineral Marines: "Silver in our hair, gold in our teeth, and lead in our butts!"

27 December 1967

"That's Marble Mountain, First Sergeant."

The company driver was giving me the scoop about the surrounding area on my way to the Third Amphibian Tractor Battalion, Fleet Marine Force, Vietnam.

"It's a national religious shrine. There's a monastery half way up those stairs," he said as he pointed toward the mountain.

Marble Mountain rises about 125 meters above us and is located just outside the gate of Amtracs* compound. The village of Nui Kim Son is at the base.

"This is the spot the first mine got one of our trucks. We sweep the road every morning now before we use it."

Marble Mountain has a monastery half way up, hundreds of caves and tunnels inside. At night the village children go into the caves to sleep, and also some of the women, in case the Viet Cong (VC) decide to shoot up our area.

"See that hooch?" said the driver as he pointed toward a small native hut. "That's one of the spots we drew fire from one night when I was on reaction patrol."

During the day the village seems quiet. Dirtier than other Asian countries I have seen. Japan is the cleanest as far as I'm concerned. There are a few shops, and one can buy marble statues or a marble desk sign. Only problem is that the "ville" is off-limits to the troops. There is supposed to be no walking through town. Around many of the huts (or hooches, as the troops call them) is a small hole or bunker.

*See Glossary

That is where the family sleeps at night. It is a lot safer than being shot at during a fire fight at night. The people do not seem overly friendly but the kids wave like they do in most countries, and the driver waves to a girl he probably sees when he is on patrol.

"This is it, First Sergeant," says the driver as the jeep comes to a stop inside the Amtracs Compound. And I am home – Headquarters and Service Company, Third Amphibian Tractor Battalion, Fleet Marine Force.

"Of all the companies I did not want, it was a Heat and Steam," I mutter half aloud. I was supposed to be assigned to a Battalion as a Sergeant Major since I was a selectee awaiting promotion. But Amtracs needed a "First" for "Heat and Steam," and I was selected. The battalion assignment will come after my promotion. In the meantime, "make the best of it, old salt."

The Battalion is located on the beach, just south of Marble Mountain. It would even be a bit picturesque, white sand, rolling surf, and a few palm trees. But a war happens to be in the area. On one side of the compound is a small fishing village and a leprosy hospital. They are between us and an Army special forces unit. On the other side we are tied in with a Navy radio transmitter station called Sea Anchor. To our front is the village called Nui Kim Son, and to our back is the ocean. Around the area are two rows of barbed wire and bunker positions. The area is considered secure during the daylight hours. At night the villagers are on curfew and we close the gate. When Charlie (VC/NVA)* opens up it is normally at night. He fires from the mountain and the villes. Last time Charlie wounded three Marines during a fire fight. Also, lobbed in some mortar rounds. One went through a hooch damaging a Marine's TV set. Charlie really knows how to hurt a guy!

*See Glossary

The monastery is a sanctuary; we are not supposed to fire at it. But Charlie uses the mountain at times and the monastery catches hell. The Colonel has been put on report twice because his Marines have fired at it. But the Marines always claim that they had been fired on first. Patrols go out at all hours of the day and night. And each morning the road through the ville is cleared for mines, starting from our gate. So far two trucks have hit a mine outside the gate, one of the drivers being killed.

The Marines live in hooches. About eight or more to a hooch. Many have TVs in the hooch. There is a chapel for church services and a recreation hut for working out, drawing sporting gear and some paperback novels. The mess hall is large and being fixed up all the time. At night movies are shown there. One incoming shell hit the corner of the mess hall, but it is repaired now.

There are various hooches for the different staff sections, officer and staff NCO* living quarters. Also, an enlisted club, officers club, and staff NCO club. Almost living garrison style, with all the comforts, even showers. But the water has to be trucked in every day, we have no wells yet. By morning we will be dry.

Marble Mountain dominates the area. Almost straight up, sort of majestic looking. Would even be picturesque – except for Charlie.

*See Glossary

10

28 December 1967

The Marine was being transferred to a stateside hospital on the West Coast. I was going through his Service Record Book, checking the entries for the Commanding Officer's signature.

The Marine had enlisted in the Midwest, took his recruit training at San Diego. When he was at Camp Pendleton for advanced infantry training, he deserted. At least a desertion report went out. Caught by civilian authorities, he was returned to military control for court-martial. He had a few more marks in his book to make it interesting reading. Not what we would call a good Marine.

The night Charlie hit, he was at one of the bunkers facing the fishing village. Charlie was sending a lot of lead from that village and the bunker was on the receiving end.

The return fire from the bunker was too low, the Marine was firing from a low position. It was ineffective; he picked up the machine gun and moved to a higher level. Holding the machine gun, he tried to rake the hooches fronting him. That was when he was hit. An enemy round shattered his wrist. He got himself a Purple Heart medal and a trip to the States.

You wonder, will he change? What kind of a civilian will he be? Or is he good only in a fire fight? Was he a good Marine? Not by his record book, but then he probably was a good man to have in a battle.

I closed the book and put it on the Skipper's desk for signing. I picked up another SRB. New man. Clean book. Wonder what kind of a Marine he is?, I thought.

11

29 December 1967

South Vietnam, long and narrow like California, compares in size to Washington State.

It is almost 600 air miles from its southern tip to the seventeenth parallel, the demarcation line set in 1954 between the northern and southern portions of the country. At its narrowest point in the north, as little as twenty-five miles lie between the coast of Vietnam and the Laotian border.

The nation has 1,500 miles of coastline and 900 miles of interior border with Cambodia and Laos.

The country is divided into three general geographical areas: delta, coastal plain, central highlands.

The first, the delta, includes all of the southern portion of the country and extends north of Saigon. Populated by more than half of the sixteen million pople of South Vietnam, it is both the chief rice-producing area and the center of industry and commerce.

In the delta, there are about 4,000 miles of navigable waterways, both rivers and canals, including the lower portion of the Mekong River that rises in Tibet and flows 2,500 miles through Asia to the South China Sea.

The second area is the coastal plain that extends north in a narrow strip along the coast from the east of Saigon. It is densely populated and heavily cultivated. The narrow fertile plain is bounded on the east by coves and beaches and on the west by plateaus of rolling land and hills.

Paralleling the coastal plain are the central highlands, broken by a chain of rugged mountains and hills. Dense jungle and forest cover much of the highlands.

Forested areas have an unbroken continuity of tall trees that form a dense, closed canopy. Underneath, an impenetrable mass of smaller growth forms one or two additional canopies.

Just north of the Equator, Vietnam has a climate typically tropical. There are two main seasons – hot and dry and hot and wet.

Because of the range of geographic features, there are wide differences in local conditions. In the south, the wet season generally runs from mid-April to mid-October. In the north, the rain begins in September and lasts through January.

When arriving in Vietnam, we are taught to respect the native customs, traditions, and religion. Do not shoot up the temples or destroy the graves of ancestors. Respect the native beliefs. The Marines try, but sometimes it is mighty hard.

The tracked landing vehicles (LVTs) from one of our companies had been going on a path between some graves in their area of operations when the mine went off, wounding the driver and causing quite a bit of damage. Charlie knew the vehicles would not go through the graveyard, so as the vehicles were channeled between the graves, he placed his mines in the best position.

The Company Gunnery Sergeant, on his second tour of duty in Vietnam, was suspicious. He ordered the remaining vehicles side to side and drove through the graveyard, tearing the graves apart. Many graves in Vietnam are about eighteen inches high, small mounds of earth.

Afterwards the Marines dug through the graves. Not one body, not a bone, nothing. Charlie had made a dummy grave site, knowing the vehicles would not go through, and had planted his mine where the vehicles would have to travel.

Sort of like fighting a war with the deck stacked against you. Sometimes it is hard for Marines to respect those customs, traditions, religions, and graveyards.

3 January 1968

I was on my way to the First Marine Division Headquarters on the other side of Da Nang. As our jeep neared a main crossroad on our route, near a place called China Beach, my driver asked, "First Sergeant, have you seen Lily?"

"No, I haven't," I replied, "This is only my second trip along here." So the driver told me about Lily.

Lily is a prostitute who lives in one of the villes near the crossroads. When the vehicles go by, Lily can sometimes be seen waving and motioning to the men. She is very informal about the whole affair. Sometimes she will lift her skirt as troops drive by. All of a sudden, my driver honked and shouted, "There she is, Top!"

My eyes were hardly in focus when I spotted her as we drove by, but enough to tell she had on the shortest mini-skirt in history – just a little lower than a belt!

On the way back, Lily was not there. My driver was disappointed not to see this famous landmark, and so was I. It was a bit unbelievable the first time and I wanted to be sure I saw what I thought I saw.

"You should have seen Lily the day the Chaplain's driver stopped by – with the Chaplain. The driver knew what would happen but the Chaplain didn't. Lily lifted her dress to show the Chaplain the wonders of the Orient, and the Chaplain almost fell out of his jeep!"

Lily is some landmark. Would not surprise me if she becomes as famous as Marble Mountain.

5 January 1968

There's going to be a memorial dispensary in the ville of Nui Kim Son. It is being built with donations for the memory of Marine rifleman, Corporal Leonard R. St. Clair (Beaumont, Texas), killed while serving with the Third Battalion, First Marines, not too far from here.

When Corporal St. Clair's parents learned of his death, they asked that friends donate money rather than flowers to a memorial for their son in Vietnam. A total of over $600 was sent to the Third Battalion. Due to operational commitments, the Third Battalion was unable to complete the project and they asked the civil affairs officer of Marine Aircraft Group-16 if he would do so.

Once completed, the dispensary will have a staff health worker, and rooms for examinations and treatment. Medical assistance will be provided by Marine Air Group-16, the Fifth Communications Battalion, our battalion of Third Amtracs, and a medical team from the Army's First Logistical Command.

Villagers worked with the Marines in constructing the memorial. A marble plaque is being made as a permanent marker to remind the villagers that a deceased Marine is the catalyst for their new health program.

6 January 1968

It is the only one in this area, for miles around. The Colonel was impressed when he heard about it. Also, some of the visitors from other outfits. The sight is remembered and the story is told.

"I'll be damned, a real one."

"Haven't seen one in months."

"Where did you get it?"

"Let's hear it again."

It sits in a small room of its own at the staff NCO club of the Third Amtracs, near Nui Kim Son. When the unit first moved into the area, the staff NCOs used a bombed-out beach house for their club while the camp was being built. Later, they built themselves a club on the beach. When it was finished they hunted, scrounged, found, and installed, "a real, gen-u-wine, stateside flush toilet!"

7 January 1968

We were standing alert. It was two o'clock in the morning, the alert had been sounded and all hands were manning the line or at their various posts. I was in the Company office, waiting to send more men if needed.

"You should have seen me, First Sergeant. I ran right into the cactus by the club," said the company armorer. He had been promoted to the rank of Staff Sergeant the day before.

It is a tradition in the Corps that when a Marine is promoted, he "wets down his stripes." He buys drinks for his friends, those he leaves and those he joins. And that first "rocker" in the Corps is a big change for a Noncommissioned Officer.

Our new Staff Sergeant went to the staff NCO club and bought his drinks. The bars close early here, so after it closed, a few NCOs decided to stay and play poker. Among them was our new Staff Sergeant. It was one o'clock in the morning when the three grenades went off. Number Six Bunker was hit, causing minor wounds to two of the three Marines on duty there. At this time, the poker players decided to leave the club, rather hastily! Having never been to the club before, and, having arrived during daylight hours, our new Staff Sergeant was lost when he came out into the night.

"Yes sir, ran right smack into that cactus," said our new Staff Sergeant. "The Mess Sergeant helped me find my way back. Seems funny now, but it sure wasn't at the time." So I gave him some advice. "Next time you better make a daylight reconnaissance of the area."

"You're right, First Sergeant, you sure are right."

9 January 1968

The young Corporal had no statement to make. He had given a written one at the investigation. The Company Commander and I were at Battalion Headquarters because the Marine was from our Company. The Sergeant Major had just marched the Marine in, and the Colonel asked him if he had any statement to make.

"I have read your statement," said the Colonel. "Would you care to repeat it to me to be sure I have read it correctly?"

"Yes, Sir," and the Marine told his story.

The Marine, a Corporal, had been in charge of an ambush patrol one night outside the wire. His patrol instructions were to set up an all-night ambush for the VC. After the Corporal placed his Marines in position, a noise was heard where no Marine was supposed to be. Thinking it was the VC, some of the patrol members fired. It was one of their own men. He had moved out of position and wandered into the "kill zone." He told his buddies in the patrol to say the VC shot him, he didn't want any Marines to be blamed. The Corporal talked it over with the patrol and they decided to claim it was enemy action. Upon return to camp, the Corporal made his report. It was a false report. Next day, on his own, he decided to correct his report and make a true statement. Now he faced the Colonel for final action on his case.

"You stepped forward on your own?" questioned the Colonel.

"Yes, Sir."

"The control of your squad was poor."

The Corporal, as a squad leader, must have complete control of his squad at all times. He may be called upon to make quick decisions at any moment. They must be the right decisions. The Corporal made an error, corrected it later, but he made a wrong decision. Now he was man enough to step forward and admit it. Marines get killed in war, and sometimes it has been friendly fire that killed them. War *is* hell, and accidents do happen. No need for a false report. An unfortunate accident, but it was not his fault. A Marine had wandered into the wrong area after he had been placed in position by the patrol leader. Fortunately, the Marine was only wounded – seriously, but he was recovering in the hospital.

For a false report, "Reduction to the rank of Lance Corporal," said the Colonel. "Considering the excellent service record of the Corporal, his performance of duty, and based on recommendations of others," the Colonel continued, "the sentence is suspended for a period of three months."

"Is that understood?" said the Colonel as he looked the Corporal hard into the eyes.

"Yes, Sir," replied the Corporal, and a very slight look of relief seemed to pass over his face.

"You showed the mark of a man when you stepped forward and corrected an error. Use better judgment from now on."

"Yes, Sir."

"About face," ordered the Sergeant Major. "March out."

There is a young Corporal in this Battalion that has the mark of a man upon him. A man among many men in this Battalion of Marines.

21

10 January 1968

During World War II it was a quonset hut. I remember moving into one of the first built in Japan after the war.

"Man, this is really living."

In Korea, I remember the squad and command post (CP) tents – especially the "warm-up" tent that first winter. You would come in after a few hours on sentry duty to thaw out.

"Man, this is really living."

I am used to foxholes, tents, or huts. In Vietnam, I learned the word hooch or hootch. I was talking to one of my Sergeants about his "hut" when he looked at me like I was a square – or a retread. The Sergeant brought me up to date. In our Company, each hooch was made to hold ten Marines.

The Skipper, the Gunny and I were inspecting hooches. Most of the Marines had regulation cots with rubber air mattresses, but some of the more enterprising, or with more horse trading abilities, had metal beds. Each Marine tried to fix a living area in his hooch. One motor transport Marine had a corner of a hooch. In his corner was a small beach chair, a floor mat, a built-in shelf and a couple of mount-out boxes for a table stand. The boxes were set sideways to make shelves, and the open end was covered by camouflage material that acted as curtains.

"Man, this is really living."

Somehow, the supplymen seem to have metal beds and the most mount-out boxes for furniture. Each hooch has one thing in common. Playgirls! Betty Grable was the girl in World War II and Marilyn Monroe did well for Korea. But this war has the Playgirl of the month. There are pictures of other girls but the ones from *Playboy* magazine are in the lead. There are no movie queens and I saw only one television star. One Marine had a photograph of Gomer Pyle above his rack (or pad). To each his own!

❀

13 January 1968

The Reaction Squad was going out on patrol this afternoon, so I decided to go along since all my clerks and the Supply Sergeant are on the Reaction Squad.

Now why would a forty-year-old First Sergeant go on patrol with a squad of Marines when he did not have to go? It has been seventeen years since my last patrol – Korea, 1950. I was a Corporal then, and much younger.

H&S Company* provides the Reaction Squad for the Battalion. It is composed of the Marines from "Heat and Steam." I believe it exemplifies the doctrine of the Corps – all Marines are riflemen first and specialists second.

The Squad Leader is Sergeant Fredrick Rabenort, the Company Supply Sergeant. Rabenort is from Minneapolis, and has been in the Marine Corps since 1965. He has been in Vietnam since March of 1966, extending his tour twice. He will be due to go back to the States in four months.

His assistant is Sergeant Billy Tidwell, the Chief Clerk for the Company. (While on patrol, I have to keep my eye on him because he is my right hand in the Company office.) Tidwell is from Houston, Texas. He originally enlisted for two years, but extended his enlistment for another year, and his tour in Vietnam for six more months. His wife lives in Houston. Corporal Timothy Telzrow, another of the Company office clerks, comes from Cleveland, Ohio, and is due to return stateside in two months.

*See Glossary

Corporal Alfred Stubbs is from the big town, Chicago, and goes home in another month, the last man in the Company office. There is also a boxer named Scott and a Marine named King.

Lance Corporal King is a Canadian. He served about ten years in the Royal Canadian Air Force and decided to enlist in the Marine Corps. He just made the age limit – almost too old. He enlisted at the Marine Recruiting Office in Seattle, and I was his recruiter. Small world!

The Patrol Leader gives instruction to the twelve other Marines in the squad, and we move out of the Battalion area. Just outside the front gate the radio gives out, and we have to wait fifteen minutes while we get a new one. The radio operator for this patrol is the Company driver, Lance Corporal Steve Christensen. He just came off two weeks of guard duty and patrolling, and was looking for a day off.

We get a new radio and move out. Our first village is Nui Kim Son, right outside the gate. The natives quietly watch as we pass through. We come to the main road, the main supply route (MSR), and turn left. Down the road to another village. The squad keeps spread out.

First check point, radio position. "Echo, this is Echo Five. We have reached our first check point." We radio in to the COC (Combat Operations Center) bunker our position at certain times. These are check points so Battalion knows where we are.

We go through the small village, past a couple of old French bunkers. As we pass, we wonder how many Legionnaires are buried in the fields of old Indochina.

"That's the hole from the mine that got the truck last week," one of the Marines remarks.

We are on the old French Road going toward Sea Anchor, the Navy radio station next to our position. Last week a mine blew up one of their trucks and injured eight men, two of them seriously.

We leave the road now and start across country – sometimes referred to as "Indian country." There are many native graves through here. We see bullet scars on many a headstone.

Sometimes Charlie sets booby-traps along here. We call it "Booby-Trap Hill." We always think of them – and the mines. Down the hill now and along the trail through the heavy brush. What a spot for an ambush! Can't see much in front or to the sides at times. It is "hairy" at night. Good spot for Charlie to hit at night. Now we come out of the brush and cross along the dikes through a rice field.

There are times Charlie plants booby-traps on the side of the dikes, and then fires. If you jump off and into the paddy, you may land on a booby-trap. So, if Charlie fires a few rounds, this old man will fall down on the trail. None of that off-the-road bit for me! I've been the rice paddy route before.

Coming to the village now. Darn thing is half-hidden in the brush, and among the trees. We see women and children, but very few men. The houses are grouped and spread out. A thick vegetation, like hedges, and bamboo and trees separate many of them, and they sit in their own little square surrounded by all the brush. As we leave the village, a group of women carrying produce of some kind approaches us on the trail, so we stop to let them pass.

As we leave the village some of the children start to follow us. "Hey, Joe," they yell, asking for candy. We have to stop the patrol while some of the Marines chase them off.

Angry because they are being chased off, one of them swears and yells, "Marines, number ten!" Number ten is very bad. Wonder where that kid learned some of his quaint English swear words? They do pick it up.

Passing through a wooded area now. Sort of like pine trees, only not very high. The ground is getting sandy again. Means we are going toward the beach now.

"There's a fishing village over there, First Sergeant," the Squad Leader points in the direction of the village and slows down the squad.

All along the route Charlie can open up on us, as he has at times on other patrols. But usually it is at night when he comes out of hiding around here and throws lead at you. That guy in the field back there – you wonder what he does for a living at night.

The squad approaches the fishing village now. Some of the natives come out to ask for gifts, women and children, no men. The kids start to collect and follow the last Marine on the squad.

As I pass through the village many of them notice my pistol, rank insignia, and probably my age. They say, "Honcho." In Korean, it meant number one man, the boss. I guess it means the same here. I am the Honcho.

Old ladies smile showing rotten teeth and betel nut stains all over their mouths. The kids in this village are brats. We cannot shake them off the last man, but they leave us at the village line.

The village is behind us now. We are on the beach and it is just a short hike back to our area. It has been an interesting three-hour walk.

Started out in a drizzle. Now it is warm and humid and almost everyone has a wet spot around the arm pits, the back, and where any equipment may be hanging. From cool and wet to hot and humid in a few hours – that's Vietnam.

The patrol is finished, so it is back to the Company for a while and then the Reaction Squad will go out and spend the night with a Marine unit in one of the villages.

So, now I have been on patrol. What was it like? Routine, I guess. After twenty-four years of soldiering, one type or another, it seems a bit routine. The feeling at forty is more relaxed than it was at twenty.

The average age of this squad is probably twenty. They are good and know their business. Some of them have been hit while on patrol, so they know the score. You can tell they like to see an old salt along. It gives them a bit of confidence, so you do not want to fail them if the chips are down. It has been said that "the old salt is the anchor in the line," and maybe he is.

They know, and I know, that a First Sergeant is not supposed to go on patrols, but it does not happen every day, and I think some of them liked it. Thirteen young Marines on patrol, and an old salt thinking, "Hell, these rice paddies smell no different than the ones in Korea."

14 January 1968*

Had to send twenty-four extra men to wire last night. Same tonight but they can sleep in their holes.

15 January 1968*

Men on line again tonight. Another truck hit a mine on Old French Road, almost same place as last week. One Vietnamese native killed, others wounded.

*From my Journal. JWJ

16 January 1968

Rumor is we may be hit in Da Nang area before Tet, Vietnamese New Year. One hundred percent alert, all hands in holes, can sleep but ready for action.

There was a total of 2,816 North Vietnam Army and Viet Cong soldiers killed throughout the I Corps area – Marine territory – during the month of December 1967. The Marines accounted for 680 enemy kills; the Army's Americal Division claimed 1,043; the RVN Army claimed 958, and the American and RVN special forces killed 100. The Republic of Korea's Second Marine Brigade added thirty-five.

In the air during December 1967, the First Marine Aircraft Wing aviators flew 5,712 fighter-attack sorties to drop 12,052 tons of ordnance. They also flew 1,205 missions over North Vietnam.

Helicopter crews flew 28,762 sorties lifting 39,394 troops and 5,448 tons of cargo while performing 10,526 tasks. There were 4,489 armed helicopter escort sorties.

According to Military Assistance Command, Vietnam (MACV) statistics for 1967 are 87,534 enemy dead. The total of the enemy dead is the equivalent of more than 114 NVA battalions.

Americans killed in action (KIAs) for 1967 were 15,997.

17 January 1968

It was 2000 hours when the field telephone rang. I was in the Company office reading up on "First Sergeanting" after a few years away from it.

I picked up the telephone, "First Sergeant."

"Hello, Top?" It was the Company Gunny on the other end. "I just got word we're going on one hundred percent alert at ten-thirty tonight. All hands, including cooks will man the line. I'll be down to the Company at ten."

That was it. Battalion put us on one hundred percent alert. Rumor is we would be hit – maybe. Figure Charlie may try a big blast before Tet, the Viet New Year.

It is 2230 hours and the Companies are moving into their holes. The comments are not those we hear in the war movies. "It's good duty, ain't it?"

The First Provisional Platoon is moving out and someone calls, "Killer, killer." Second Provisional Platoon moves out for the line. The weather is cool, some Marines are carrying their poncho liners or a blanket. It is a sleeping watch, they can take turns sleeping in their holes. The bunker positions are manned by the permanent guard force and stay awake. Here come the cooks and messmen. Half are sent with one platoon and half are sent with the other. The Marines kid about it being total war – "Must be tough, the cooks are going on line."

Everyone is in their holes. I am at the Company office with a reserve force. The reserve is in the bunker behind me.

If anything happens I can take the reserve force to where needed.

About eleven o'clock at night the telephone rings. The cooks are to come off the line at five in the morning so they can fix chow. I go out to find the Mess Sergeant. He is sleeping by one of the bunkers. I wake him up and give him the word. He's getting too old to be sleeping in a hole.

"OK, First Sergeant," he says, and then lets out a wheezing cough.

"Better try and get behind the bunker. You've got a bad cold," I tell him. A breeze is coming in off the ocean, getting colder. "It will help keep some of the wind off."

Six in the morning. Everyone comes off the line, cleans up and goes to work by zero seven-thirty. We are to go one hundred percent alert again tonight. Probably be another dry run.

It is not even dark when Charlie fires at one of our patrols. I put on my flak jacket, helmet, grab my pistol, and head for the Company office. Other Marines are doing the same. I hear a few "zings" overhead. I can see it now, another night of one hundred percent alert.

"Damn you, Charlie!"

23 January 1968

The last time I saw the Gunny was at Camp Pendleton in 1963 – it was his retirement. After twenty plus years in the Corps, he was going to hang it up in a seabag. There was no parade or ceremony, the Gunny wanted to go quietly. So we had some coffee in the Colonel's office and shot the breeze about the Gunny's future plans.

We did not say goodbye when he left; it is a small world and Marines always seem to run into each other later on. So he left with a handshake and "I'll be seeing you, Top."

"So long, Gunny," I replied.

About six months after he retired I received a telephone call at home one evening. It was the Gunny calling from El Paso, Texas. He would rather talk than write letters. Two years later he telephoned me again. I was on recruiting duty in Seattle, Washington, when he called my office. Postage is cheaper but he likes to telephone.

It was about this time that the Fifth Marine Division was being activated at Camp Pendleton to meet the Corps requirements for Vietnam. We had two divisions over there and none on the West Coast. The call went out to the retired list asking for volunteers to return to active duty. The Gunny was among those that answered the call.

I was on my way to Hill 65, near Di Loc, with gear and mail for some of our Marines. The road south from our area had not been cleared yet so we drove back to Da Nang and then south again on another road. We had just passed the Da Nang airstrip and, as we turned a corner, I noticed a

Marine waiting to cross the road. He looked familiar. I told my driver to stop.

"Hold it, Chris." Getting out of the jeep I yelled, "Hey, Gunny!"

When he looked he was not sure at first; it had been almost five years since he retired. The Gunny was going on R&R* and was waiting for his flight, due to go out in two hours. He just happened to be walking around the area. We shot the breeze for a little while and then I had to leave. It was a handshake and, "I'll be seeing you, Gunny."

"So long, Top."

As I got back in the jeep I told my driver to "Shove off, Chris," and thought to myself, "It *is* a small world."

*See Glossary

24 January 1968

The old warhorse heard the sound of the bugle and trotted off to battle.

It was about four-thirty in the afternoon when the word was passed. "Reaction Squad and tractors down to the COC bunker, now!"

That pretty well wiped out the Company Headquarters section and some of the Battalion offices.

The Reaction Squad is my Marines – well, I sort of feel that way about them since those I know best are in it. They always offer an invitation to the old warhorse to go along. I went with them to the command bunker to see what it was all about. Second time this week. The COC bunker is built partially below ground, reinforced by timbers and covered with sandbags. It contains the communications center and combat operations room of the Battalion.

It was not quite like we see in the war movies. As I entered, my Supply Sergeant, the Reaction Squad leader, was in a heated argument with one of the Marines in the Operations Section. The verbal exchange concerned what happened to some office supplies sent to the COC. War is hell, but without paper clips it can be horrible! The Operations Officer, a Major, explained the situation:

Five LVTs (tracs), three from Bravo Company and two from H&S, will be part of a blocking force while the ARVN (Vietnamese Army) forces sweep an area. The operation will start at three in the morning. The Reaction Squad will provide security for the LVTs. The officer in charge will be a young Lieutenant from Civil Affairs Section. No one has been in the area before.

"Draw your rations, ammo, radioman, and a corpsman."

I went topside and talked to one of my office clerks, Sergeant Tidwell, the assistant squad leader.

"Why don't you go with us, First Sergeant?"

"I sure would like to, but the old man would probably say no."

"You could check with the Captain."

"He wasn't too happy about me going out last time."

The old warhorse could hear the bugles. He sort of got that old feeling – some of that gung-ho-ness. Not wanting to be left in the rear with the gear, he galloped off to see the Company Commander for permission to go.

"Can't do it," said the Captain.

"Damn it to hell why not, Skipper?"

After some hard talking the Skipper said, "OK, if the XO approves." The XO was the Battalion Executive Officer. So off galloped the old warhorse again.

"No," said the Major, "How could we justify it?"

Although the answer was "no," the bugle could still be heard. But it was no use; First Sergeants do not go with squads on patrol or small size operations. Besides, the Colonel was against it.

It was six in the evening, the tracs bellowed a roar with their engines and started through the wire at the back of the CP area. The old warhorse could see the Reaction Squad atop the tracs: Corporal Scott, the special services NCO; Corporal Malone, the Chaplain's assistant; Corporal Stubbs, who would be going home soon; Sergeants Rebenort and Tidwell, and others.

Through the exhaust, sand, and setting sun, the old warhorse sensed another feeling as the young colts rode off. I damn near cried.

26 January 1968

Queenie is the mascot for Third Amtracs. Originally scheduled for duty as a scout dog, Queenie was kept from combat duty when it was discovered that a bone ailment hampered her actions.

"We give her vitamins regularly to keep her in tip-top shape," stated Corporal Dexter Fletcher (Northeast Harbor, Maine), who cares for Queenie.

The dog was adopted for the Battalion in October of 1967 by Lieutenant Colonel Robert L. Shuford (Fallbrook, California), who was the Battalion Commander. Queenie has been accorded some privileges; she rides up front in the Colonel's jeep, eats and sleeps in the Colonel's quarters. She follows the new Battalion Commander, Lieutenant Colonel Robert E. Haebel (Media, Pennsylvania), on his tours of the Battalion area.

Also, Queenie has assigned herself the duty of being an unofficial Battalion greeter. "She usually makes the rounds of the staging area whenever any of the guys are going out on a mission or when they're returning," said Corporal Fletcher. "I know the guys enjoy seeing her. They look upon it as sort of a good luck thing," he added.

Occasionally Queenie stands guard duty with her boyfriend, Clyde, a former Vietnamese sentry dog.

It is a dog's life, and Queenie is one dog that knows how to live it.

27 January 1968*

Over at the Da Nang AB Transient Center, a trio of stalwart young Marines were awaiting the big bird that would transport them back to the States after thirteen months in Vietnam.

They had been combat-hardened at places like Khe Sanh, Con Thien and a dozen operations with odd-sounding names.

But there was still something uncertain and worried in their bearings and expressions.

"I'm afraid to go home," spoke one tanned giant. "I'm too young. At least we should first get some special field training or combat orientation."

"Yeah," said another, "I hear it's pretty hairy back there – hippies in the hinterland and protestors pounding the pavements. There's not even a DMZ**. They've infiltrated the entire corps area."

The third theorized, "We need more operations out from bases like Pendleton and Lejeune and a good strong Leatherneck Square. Combined Action Platoons should be inserted in overrun hamlets like Berkeley, Ann Arbor, and Cambridge. Pacification is failing in Milwaukee, Detroit, and Chicago. Down south they should start a Chieu Hoi program. The TAOR** around Sunset Strip, Greenwich Village, and Haight-Ashbury need recon work."

"Rest at ease, gang," quoth a grizzled "First" who had edged his way up to the summit meeting. "Your G-2** is off. You're snowed by the domino-bowling pin hypothesis. So listen up.

"Do you realize that terrorist activities are few and far between? Softheaded kooks are a small minority and hard-core extremists about as scarce as horse dung on the freeways. About 99 and 44/100 percent of all Americans are solidly behind our guys over here.

"Take Christmas for example. The Wing got a 60-foot scroll signed by members of the student body at East Tennessee State. One almost like it came from the citizens of Newcastle, Pennsylvania, to the Third Marine Division.

*News item in *Sea Tiger* (no by-line printed)
**See Glossary

"Recently another greeting came in to the First Marine Division from San Jose State with 500 student signatures.

"Individuals, churches, clubs, fraternities, schools, industries – all kinds of groups, organized and disorganized, showed in the variety of ways that they were our allies. And a fine group of VIPs come out to help our morale.

"Cheer up! The infrastructure of the V.C. (virulent contumacy) is dissolving and there's progress on the home front."

The threesome picked up their bags, threw back their shoulders and with sparkling eyes, firm jaws, jaunty airs and confident gaits mounted to the airplane's cabin.

❀

30 January 1968

It was to be the "Year of the Monkey." There was to be a truce during Tet. It started at 6 pm (1800 hours) on January 29, 1968.

If that was a truce, I wonder what a peace treaty would be like?

The alert sounded and it was "All hands to the wire" (defensive positions) at 2310 hours, January 30. The truce was over and it would be a busy ten days. Many hours are spent just waiting during combat conditions.

At seven o'clock in the morning, we secured from the line. It had been quiet for us, although we could see flashes of other areas being hit. The Marine Helicopter strip two miles to our north got hit; mortars and rockets were heard. Also Da Nang Airfield got it.

The Company was beginning to muster after breakfast when the Company Commander, Captain Michael Gardner (Harrisburg, Pennsylvania), shouted to me: "Provisional Platoons One and Two to the COC bunker. On the double!"

The provisional platoons comprised all Marines that are not Amtrac crewmen – the Headquarters and Service Company supplymen, communicators, clerks, maintenance men, drivers, mechanics, and others. Heat and Steam is not considered a combat company, and at times its members are harassed about this by the "letter companies," who consider themselves the fighting Marines.

About the time I passed the word for the platoons to move out, I received another telephone call. I had just entered the

Company office. "First Sergeant here." It was the COC on the other end of the line. "Yes, Sir."

I turned to the Company Clerk. "Sergeant Tidwell, get the Reaction Squad down to COC with all its gear." He moved out to collect the squad. It consisted of all the company clerks, supply sergeant, embarkation clerk, a cook and five others. The Skipper came in, grabbed a helmet, ordered the cooks and messmen to COC, jumped in a jeep, and departed in a cloud of dust.

A few miles from our area the infantry had some VC or NVA trapped on an island, and our Amtracs and Marines were to act as a blocking force.

Heat and Steam was going into action, less Marines and tracs, with the Korean Marines and the Seventh Marine Regiment. By the time I hit the tractor park, cooks, messmen, clerks, crewmen, and the provisional platoons were climbing aboard the tracs. I reported to the Skipper and got the word. I was to stay at the CP and man the defense.

Another operation and I got to stay in the rear. "Might as well retire," I said. A few more choice words to myself and I started to count what I had to muster. The Reaction Squad went down the road to guard prisoners. I had twenty-eight Marines left in the Company, about half of them were staff NCOs.

At ten o'clock in the morning it was one hundred percent alert and all available Marines, including staff NCOs, to the wire. It was warm outside by now; it was going to be a long hot day. The galley was empty, all cooks and messmen had gone aboard the tracs. Beats mess duty! "Will have to issue Cs" (C-rations).

It was one hundred percent alert all night. Up and down H&S sector I went. "Stay awake, Marine!" By morning I was tired. We secured the line by ten o'clock – twenty-four hours on watch.

The blocking force was in action. Corporal James Malone (Omaha, Nebraska), had made a kill when a VC came after him with a grenade. As Malone dived into the river to evade the VC, Sergeant William Harvath (Cleveland, Ohio), aboard a trac (LVT) fired a few rounds, and Malone came up smiling. Corporal Malone is the Chaplain's assistant, and Sergeant Harvath is an administrative clerk in Battalion headquarters.

One of our men was to leave for home. When the road opened, I got the Battalion mail clerk to take him to Da Nang when he went for the mail. The Marine was beginning to wonder if he would ever get out. He did. Since there was still firing along the road, I gave him a helmet and armored vest to wear down. "Send it back with the driver."

Eight o'clock in the evening, and on the line again. It would be one hundred percent alert. I was going along the line when I saw them from bunker Number One. The count was 142. The Reaction Squad and some ARVN (Army Republic Vietnam) brought them in – VC suspects. They were interrogated all night.

Two of the H&S tracs came in. The dead VC and some of their equipment were beginning to come in. "And a few more for the line," I said to myself.

It was two o'clock in the morning. Some fog was in low, and almost hid the wire. I was tired, as I'd been up and down the line every hour to be sure everyone was awake. It was still one hundred percent alert. I was sharing a hole with Corporal Fred Lounge (Columbus, Ohio) and Corporal Glenn Bulman (Bremerton, Washington), both communicators. They had been on communications watch all day. Corporal Bulman, a radio operator, had one of the radios on the COC network. "Good way to know what's going on," he said.

Flares went off, and the area lit up like day. "Charlie is in the wire." It was on the other side. "I wish they would hit

41

our side." It was Corporal Lounge; he was tired of waiting. Hit and get it over with. Charlie didn't hit our side.

The rest of the company returned in the morning.

"You should have seen them, First Sergeant; I was proud of every damn one of them." It was Staff Sergeant Mike Taylor (Staten Island, New York), telling me about the Marines in his platoon and others. "They were good, kept on going. I'm proud of them." Sergeant Taylor is the Battalion Motor Transport Chief, also Platoon Sergeant for one of the provisional platoons.

Well, Tet was over, but we had ten more days "in our holes." When it was all over, ol' Heat and Steam had three dead and seven wounded.

1 February 1968*

0200 Charlie in Sea Anchor wire.
0730 Secure from line. Accidental discharge of weapon (MG**) fatal to Sgt Cody.

4 February 1968*

0700 Off line – quiet night, only 50% alert (one asleep, one awake).
1400 Memorial Service for Sgt Cody.
1930 Out on line, 50% alert.

6 February 1968*

0240 100% alert – supposed to be an NVA BN somewhere.
1930 All hands to wire 100% alert.

7 February 1968*

0700 Off line – 2 hours sleep – normal routine. Notified six men wounded with Third Bn Seventh Marines.
1930 On line, 100% alert.

*From my Journal. JWJ
**See Glossary

7 February 1968

There were two small paper bags on my desk. I knew what they were before I opened them. The personal effects off the bodies of our two Marines killed in action (KIAs). I opened the first bag; it contained a small religious medallion, insignia of rank, and a cigarette lighter. The lighter still had blood on it; the Marine had been shot three times in the chest.

"Chris," I yelled.

"Yes, Top."

"Clean the blood off this lighter. Can't send it home like that."

Chris is Lance Corporal Steve Christensen (Boise, Idaho), the Company Driver. A good Marine.

The other bag contained eleven dollars in military script and a religious medal on a chain.

"One married, one single. Charlie plays no favorites. Chris, get the jeep. I want to go to NSA."* We have two wounded Marines there, both from the same operation. Four wounded and two dead. That platoon really got hit.

We arrived at the hospital and it was like all others in a war zone. Men sitting around, medics and corpsmen going from place to place. The stretcher bearers waiting for the 'copters to come in with the Medevacs. One right there was fresh, "Must have just arrived."

The sign on the door said Ward 5A. "He's in here."

Lance Corporal Eugene Bevill (Texarkana, Arkansas), was wounded in the left hand and below the right eye by

*See Glossary

44

shrapnel and small arms fire. The LVT he was riding on was hit while in support of an infantry unit. He saw his buddies get hit. The one with the eleven dollars on my desk was "reaching down to help a wounded grunt when he got hit."

Bevill continued the story. "I saw him straighten up when he was hit. One of the men grabbed him before he fell off the trac." He sat there a minute, quiet. He had that stare many men in many wars get when a battle or fight is still fresh in their minds, remembering what it was like, with their buddies dying around them.

Then he started to talk again. I gave him a hometown newspaper that had come in the mail and some money he had left in the company safe.

"Doc said I would be leaving for the States tomorrow."

But he did not quite believe it yet. He had a misty look in his eyes when I left. Probably glad it was over for him and yet not wanting to leave his buddies behind. I do not know; I suppose it was a look of unbelief.

The ambulance was leaving with a load of cases when I climbed aboard the jeep. Among the fringe benefits of being a First Sergeant is visiting your Marines in the hospital, identifying the KIAs, and inventorying personal effects. Someone has to do it. For my KIAs it is all over. For the Wounded in Action (WIAs), if they are lucky, it is a trip back home. For me, it will probably be more KIAs and WIAs – and more widows and heartbroken parents. That part of war has never changed.

"OK Chris, head for home."

9 February 1968

Ask any Vietnamese villager from Nui Kim Son, located five miles southwest of Da Nang, what a "county fair" is and talk of livestock shows, baking contests and greased-pig races will never enter into the conversation.

The villagers of Nui Kim Son had their own county fair last month, but the Vietnamese version of the fair was considerably different from the ones that most Americans are familiar with.

Leathernecks of the Third Amphibian Tractor Bn. and the First Military Police Bn. joined with units of the US Army and Navy, and elements of the local Vietnamese Regional and Popular Forces to conduct the two-day county fair operation.

On the first day at dawn, the allied forces moved into the village and escorted the Vietnamese to a pre-selected point in the nearby, abandoned French fort.

As the villagers started gathering, friendly forces systematically began to sweep through the area in search of hiding Viet Cong.

The villagers soon discovered that a day of fun and assistance had been set up for them to offset the inconvenience of keeping them away from their homes.

At the fort a field dispensary was opened. Navy doctors and hospital corpsmen treated any Vietnamese that needed medical assistance.

A mobile broadcasting van was located at the collection point, and throughout the day music and speeches were played for the villagers' listening enjoyment. A movie was shown that evening for their entertainment.

Toys and games were handed out to the children to keep them amused while the forces continued their search.

Many other items were distributed during the day, including soap, clothing and one ton of rice in addition to other food stuffs. An almost festive holiday atmosphere prevailed at the fair.

Understandably, the Viet Cong would have been about the only people that didn't enjoy themselves during the day. They would have been much too busy running and hiding from their relentless pursuers to have had any time for fun and games.

*News article in *Sea Tiger* by Corporal Jeff Ault

10 February 1968

Every Marine is a rifleman first. The Corps is built around this credo. But some are assigned less glamorous duties.

Corporal Raymond J. Tracy Jr. (Chicago, Illinois), is a good cook for Heat and Steam. He puts in many hours working – feeding the troops. Corporal Tracy was once a member of the Reaction Squad but had to be taken off the squad – the Mess Sergeant did not like him to be gone so often.

"I need him in the mess hall and not running off to play John Wayne."

The cooks had their day during the so-called truce. The Battalion formed a blocking force to stop Charlie from escaping from a trap during "Operation Auburn." All the cooks went aboard the tracs with the rest of Heat and Steam to chase Charlie for forty-eight hours. They came back tired, dirty, sweaty, noses peeling from sunburn, and with smiles. They got into the field for some time and felt more like Marines than cooks and bakers.

I was having my first real hot breakfast in two days. The cook with the sunburned nose, Private First Class Joseph Gigliotta (New Orleans, Louisiana) was frying eggs and seemed rather cheerful.

"Hey, First Sergeant, when we gonna get to go to the field again?"

13 February 1968

It is customary for the skipper to write a letter of condolence to the family of a Marine killed in action. After the Skipper wrote a letter to the parents of one of our KIAs and the wife of another, I sat down to write one of my own. I had some color Polaroid photographs of the memorial service held for our two KIAs and thought the parents and wife would like to have them:

> *Dear Mrs. ------------,*
>
> *Enclosed are two photographs of the memorial service conducted by our Battalion for your husband and another Marine recently killed in action.*
>
> *I know your grief is great at this time but it may help to know that when your husband was killed he was trying to help another Marine.*
>
> *He was among Marines from this company providing support to an infantry company in battle a few miles from here.*
>
> *When your husband was hit, he was reaching down from his LVT trying to pull a rifleman aboard. His LVT had gone in to try and rescue Marines.*
>
> *I thought you would like to know this.*
>
> > *Very sincerely,*
> > *JACK W. JAUNAL*
> > *1st Sgt of Marines*

48

Dear First Sergeant Jaunal,

I have received your letter and pictures and I will be forever thankful.

My husband was a hero and he was a hero to his son.

All I knew was that he was killed. I did not know how he died. Now I know. He was a hero and always will be to his son and I.

God Bless you.

Sincerely,

----

19 February 1968

A bullet sometimes leaves a small, clean wound. Normally a small hole going in. If it goes through the body, it sometimes tears the flesh off on the way out. Small hole in front, larger one in the back. Shrapnel, mines, and booby traps sometimes tear and rip into the flesh, leaving ugly scars.

It was zero two ten when I got word that two "of your men got hit by a mine." It was afternoon before the Company Commander and myself could get to the hospital to see how our wounded were doing.

"They're in Ward 1B," the corpsman told us.

Because this was not our first trip to the hospital, we knew where it was. We saw them both. They were down a few beds and across from each other. The first one was sitting up in his bed reading a magazine. He looked up and gave a small smile that said, "Am I glad to see you." I knew him pretty well – he was Private First Class Leonard C. Pratte, Jr. (Ballwin, Missouri), one of our grunts. He had not even been in the outfit a month. He was bare chested and his name was printed across his chest with iodine. There were a few blood clots on his forehead, and a large bandage on the right side of his cheek.

"I didn't know I was hit 'til I felt the hole in my cheek," he said.

His left arm from the elbow down was bandaged. Shrapnel had torn into his flesh there also. He had a look of wonder in his eyes as we talked. I noticed that his right leg would twitch every once in awhile. I asked him what happened.

"A piece of shrapnel went through my leg. I didn't even know it."

He was sure glad he was not the point man on the patrol. That was the other wounded Marine we came to visit. We chatted a little while. Small talk and we asked if there was anything he needed or we could do. I noticed the bandages were still red with blood. He said he was "OK" and we went to the bed of the other wounded Marine. He was Private First Class William T. Hukill (Treverton, Pennsylvania), and he was pretty cheerful, even if the top of his head, both arms, and his right leg were bandaged. I noticed the blood that had dried between his toes. His leg was broken, and shrapnel had pretty well torn into the flesh. He even had a few pieces in his chest.

"Wouldn't have any there," I said as I pointed to his chest, "if you had your vest (flak jacket) zipped up."

He agreed. We talked about how it happened. He was the point man and felt the booby trap wire as he stepped on it. As he looked around expecting the explosion, it came. The blast tore him up a bit, as well as the Marine behind him, and a small piece went into the chest of one of our Vietnamese scouts.

"You've got to keep off those used trails," the Skipper said.

He agreed that they had learned a lesson. They ran into the trap just off the Old French Road. It always seems to be mined or booby trapped. We had been lucky for awhile. No casualties along there for almost a month.

"Is there anything you need?" I asked.

"Yeah, could I have a soda?"

Here he was lying in the rack, bandaged almost from head to toe and what did he want? A soda! Great!

We joked about how he got hit about everywhere except his "manly parts."

51

"Yeah, I was lucky." He was.

The Captain and I said we would see them later and we left. Both would probably be evacuated to a hospital out of country.

Good Marines. Plenty of guts. They seemed kind of young, but I remembered I was about their age in World War II. And luckier!

"Yes, sir, that shrapnel is wicked stuff."

22 February 1968

It looks like another Torii* craze. The last one I remember started in 1953 when the Third Marine Division landed in Japan. It must be the "Asiatic" influence in the Corps. Units would build small Torii, and hanging from, or painted on each, would be a sign proudly proclaiming such-and-such unit.

Then I remembered the Torii at Camp Pendleton's Staging Battalion – the one which proudly proclaims that it is "The Gateway To The Orient." Many a Marine has read those words on his way overseas.

At Third Amtracs, I noticed when I arrived that there is a small Torii in front of the Combined Action Company office; rather modest with "GOLF" for Company G printed on the sign. Further through the Battalion area another sign greeted my eyes, "3d AMTRAC BN," and beneath it, "A Company." At Company B the Torii was larger, a shield hung from the top and a large Marine Corps emblem was painted on it.

For some little while it was quiet. As I walked out of the office hut one day, I found the Supply Sergeant and a Company clerk working on a rather large familiar-looking object.

"What is that? And who told you to build it anyway?"

"The CO*," was their reply.

I went down in defeat as the H&S Company Torii was raised to its majestic heights. It was the tallest Torii in the

*See Glossary

area, painted red with yellow lettering. A large red shield hung from the top, with letters a foot high proclaiming "H&S." At the top of the shield, in yellow letters three inches high, was the name of the Company Commander, my name, and the name of the Company Gunnery Sergeant. On each side of the Torii was placed a large rice jar, two feet high and painted white. It was indeed the best looking Torii in the Battalion, if not all of Vietnam.

Shortly thereafter, one was built for the Colonel, but it was not quite as tall, and no names hung from it. It is painted the same as H&S Company, red and yellow, for the Marine Corps colors of scarlet and gold.

Next time Charlie drops a round or two in the Battalion area, I hope he does not hit a Torii. I am afraid the damn things may multiply!

23 February 1968*

A provisional infantry squad of cooks, maintenance men and civil affairs personnel from Third Amphibian Tractor Bn., reinforced a company of the Third Battalion, Fifth Marine Regiment during a fierce, four-hour battle with the Viet Cong.

At 0300 hours, the Amtracs were set up as a blocking force for a routine sweeping mission across the Vinh Dien River. They received word that a platoon of Marines had come under heavy fire from an estimated force of 200 VC, and needed help.

"Twelve of us were told to board an Amtrac that took us across the river to the platoon's position," said Sergeant Ernest E. Piotrovski (Ellen Park, Michigan).

"As soon as we arrived the VC started mortaring us and we were split up and placed in defensive positions," he continued.

Several VC were killed inside the Leatherneck perimeter as the enemy launched their first human wave assault.

After 30 minutes of exchanging steady fire, the VC attempted another suicide attack. Three enemy troops came within 20 feet of Piotrovski's position before he killed them.

Again the assault was repelled as the Marines set down a heavy volume of fire.

Intense automatic weapons fire and grenade exchanges lasted until dawn, when the VC broke contact.

Three VC were captured. They had penetrated the Leatherneck defenses and hidden in a spider hole inside the Marine perimeter throughout the entire battle.

Nineteen VC dead were found. Several blood trails were also discovered, as well as a number of AK-47 assault rifles, machine guns, bangalore torpedoes and medical supplies.

*News item in *Sea Tiger* by Corporal Mike Stokey II

25 February 1968

It is about dusk. I am coming out of the mess hall with my gear in one hand and a canteen cup of hot coffee in the other. As I cross the road going toward the Company office I see the Gunny already issuing grenades to the platoons. Each Marine walks past the Gunny and is given two hand grenades and a belt of rifle ammo. I enter the Company office and the Skipper gives me the scoop. "First, it will be the same as last night. One hundred percent alert. No one sleeps! We will go to the wire at 1900 hours and come off about 0700 tomorrow."

In front of H&S Company positions are two villages. One is named Nui Kim Son; the other is a small fishing village just called, "the ville."

The Captain and the Gunny stay at Bunker One, about the center of our area of responsibility, and near the main gate. I am stationed at Bunker Four with the three regular guard sentries. An LVT with a searchlight is used for back-up at Bunker Four. Every once in awhile we shine it on the fishing ville and along our wire. We are dug in near the beach; our wire starts along the beach here. It is Company A's area after us, to our right.

It is dark now and I finish my coffee. This is going to be another long night. I turn out the office light and stumble into the night with my gear. My eyes begin to adjust to the darkness as I walk through the Company area making a last minute check. I can see the outline of the LVT and walk toward it.

"Halt! Who goes there?"
I shout, "First Sergeant, H&S, and don't give me any lip, Doc!"
I hear a laugh – it is Doc, our Navy corpsman. He stands alerts at Bunker Four with me. We are always challenging each other.

It is cool at Bunker Four. Placing my gear on the sandbags, I put on my field jacket. It is early yet so we find enough to talk about...like R&R in Hawaii and meeting our wives there.

About ten at night the talk begins to slow down. We listen to the bells ring in the monastery on Marble Mountain and watch a light move now and then. What are the VC plotting to do to us now?

Doc decides to go get some coffee at the mess hall. He comes back later with a canteen full of black hot coffee. It is good.

"Guess I will check the line," and I start for the first hole. It is getting misty now. "Going to get wet tonight." The Marines are awake and alert. Near Bunker Three I meet the Skipper; he is out checking the line also. It was at Bunker Three we had two men wounded in December. Takes me about forty-five minutes to check the line. On my way back to my bunker I stop at the mess hall for a cup of coffee. The night cook, Corporal William E. Stirman (Midland, Texas), looks up and greets me.

"How many gallons of coffee have you made tonight?" I ask.

"About forty-five gallons," he replies.

"That's a lot of coffee. How many last night?"

"Ninety gallons."

"We may beat it tonight, it's early yet."

We drink a lot of coffee to stay awake these nights. Marines come to the galley all night to get coffee. They fill their canteens and take it back for themselves and their buddy in the hole.

When I get back to the bunker it is quiet. The ville is dark and has been all night. Strange, the little shrines are not even lit tonight.

Midnight and it starts to rain. I put on my flak vest. If it is good enough to stop shrapnel, it is good enough to stop rain. It takes some time for the chill between my shoulders to go away. My jacket was too damp. After an hour or so it dries out and the vest helps keep me warm.

I have been standing in the pit and against the sandbags for two hours. My chin has been resting on a sandbag while I watch the village for the last thirty minutes. My eyes get tired and heavier all the time.

"We'll need toothpicks to keep our eyes open, Doc."

He agrees with me and we chat a bit.

Three o'clock in the morning. There's a song about that. "Guess I'll check positions," and I head for the first hole.

"How goes it, Marine?"

"Rough," replies the Marine, "but at least it stopped raining."

Good Marines. Work all day and stay up all night. Two, maybe three hours sleep in the morning and all over again. How many nights? Last time it was ten.

As I approach one hole I notice the Marine is sitting on the edge of the sandbags, feet hanging in the hole. He keeps rocking back and forth. I stand beside him for a little while. His buddy has fallen asleep sitting up in the hole. This one is trying to stay awake. His head falls forward and about the time I think he will fall on his face his head comes back up and he balances. I place my right hand on his shoulder and shake him.

"Don't you think at least one of you should stay awake?"

His eyes come into focus and he looks at me questioningly for a moment.

"Yeah, First Sergeant. Must be trying to doze off."

I finish another forty-five minute tour and am beginning to drag my anchor.

Four-thirty and I doubt I can stay awake. I put my poncho liner around me. Damp sea breeze and wind.

Five o'clock and I sit down. No movement in the ville.

Five-thirty and I stand and walk around the bunker.

Six o'clock. Some movement in the ville. Fishing boats go out.

Six-thirty. Starting to wake up again.

Seven o'clock. "Pass the word to secure. Chow till eight-thirty. Work day starts at noon."

As I stand at Bunker Four, wrapped up like an Indian chief inside my poncho, I can see the Marines move out of their holes. Tired, unshaven, and red-eyed from lack of sleep after two nights of nonsleep. They head for the mess hall and breakfast.

"Good duty," some of them quip.

I pick up my gear and head in the same direction. It will be the same routine tonight. I can hardly wait!

1 March 1968

One of our trac mechanics, Lance Corporal John C. Fritch (Dallas, Texas), got away from his regular duty as a mechanic and became a gunner.

Fritch was a member of a provisional infantry squad formed to reinforce some Amtracs that were blocking an area during a routine sweep for VC south of here.

"Shortly after we arrived, we received word that a squad of Marines was under heavy enemy fire across the river from us," stated Fritch.

The Marines under fire had already taken a casualty and wanted the LVT to come over and help evacuate the wounded. As his LVT reached the opposite side of the river, Fritch, who was manning a .30 caliber machine gun aboard the LVT, came under enemy fire.

"I tried to lay down a base of fire so the Marines could get the casualty to us, but an enemy machine gun position kept them from moving," he later stated.

Fritch then told the crew chief to move the LVT in front of a hedgerow which blocked a view of the enemy position. As the LVT plowed through the treeline, Fritch opened fire on the enemy gun position, killing one of the Viet Cong. Another VC attempted to fire the enemy gun and Fritch killed him.

Now mechanic Fritch is back to his normal routine duty.

❀

26 March 1968

There are many duties that are performed in the field or under combat conditions that are unpleasant, but necessary. One of them is cleaning "heads." "Heads" are Navy terminology and are required for civilized man. When on the move a Marine can dig his own, a small hole, squat, and then bury his waste. When he is in the CP area, he will have the military version of the "outhouse."

We use the "four holer." Under each one is a sawed off half of a fifty-five gallon drum. Fuel oil is in the bottom of each barrel half. Each morning a "head detail" of two Marines cleans all the company heads and burns inside the barrels. Each barrel is removed from the head and another is set in its place. Fuel oil is poured on the waste and each barrel is burned clean and any ashes buried. The next morning the process is repeated. One of the many duties a Marine may be required to perform – not glamorous or gung-ho, but necessary.

The Battalion tried to hire Vietnamese to clean the heads. The Company Gunny took the first two hired and showed them what to do. They looked, shook their heads, and walked out the gate. The next two were so old it was doubtful they could lift the barrels. They looked, shook their heads, and walked out the gate. The Vietnamese would not do the job.

So we still have our "Head Captain."

27 March 1968

Once a wingwiper, grunt, tracrat, or some other breed of Marine life digs in for any period of time, he begins to homestead. He begins to improve his living conditions at the earliest opportunity. This is when the "individual touch" stands out among the uniformity of the military.

Take the showers for instance. Our Battalion has four. Each one is an individual; none are alike or uniform. Each is housed in a small hut, but the system that heats the water is the craftsmanship of pioneers. The heat for the Officers and Staff NCO shower is provided by a fifty-five gallon barrel set on a stand about four feet high. Fuel oil (diesel) is turned on by a knob mounted on a pipe from the drum. The pipe ends over the open top of another fifty-gallon barrel. The fuel is turned on and it drops to the bottom of the empty barrel. Inside is a coil of pipes that carries the water to the shower. Once the fuel starts in the barrel it is lighted and the water starts to heat. The more fuel, the hotter the water, or the faster it starts to heat. The water heated, you now run inside and turn on the shower. The shower must be on or the safety faucet turned on. If not, steam builds up and —! If the pipes are too hot you get steam, but once the steam is out, hot water.

Now the trick is to get the right combination of hot and cold water together. This can be tricky at times, especially when one or two more persons enter the shower. First, one may take more hot water and all of a sudden your shower is cold. Or off goes a shower and you leap from under too much hot water. The first time I entered the shower on my own, I leaned my head too far under the shower as the first batch of steam and water came out. I had forgotten to open the safety faucet. It is a rather painful way to learn proper "care and feeding" of a temperamental shower.

When finished with showering, the last man must turn off the fuel and leave the safety faucet on. Eventually the fire goes out, the water turns cold and the first one hearing the water running goes in and turns it off, if cold.

Water is trucked in every day by three tanker trucks. Water is supposed to be conserved. The water is stored in a large tank on a tower above the mess hall. It travels downhill to the company showers, Company A being first. Therefore when our shower is empty, Company A is still going strong. Company A has a large tank set about eight feet off the ground. The fuel is in a bed along the side of the tank, the tank being lengthwise. The operation of all the showers is basically the same. When Company A first set off their heating element it looked as if the entire shower would burn down. Company A has a large fire, but it is because of the size of their water tank.

Company B for some reason seems to be popular with many Marines from other companies. Maybe it is because the shower always seems to be working. Company B uses the fifty-five gallon fuel drum and a pipe into a water storage tank set on the ground in a fuel tank.

Heat and Steam has the most elaborate of all showers with a large fuel pipe and a turning knob almost the size of a freight car brake wheel. We, H&S, have the largest hottest fire of all. From a distance it looks like a building on fire.

Gunny built a shower using jet fuel as the fuel for heating. Of course you could not have the fire and fuel going at the same time. The day of "blast off" the Gunny lit the heater. Half the Company came to see if it would work, the other half came to see "the Gunny get killed." It worked! Of course, flames leaped hundreds of feet into the air, but the water was HOT. That is American know-how at work.

Next to a hot meal and mail from home, a good old hot shower cannot be beat.

1 April 1968

The Battalion was beginning to form up, less those Marines in the field and on duty. I was standing in the doorway of the Company office watching H&S march into position. Soon it would be over.

My thoughts rolled back over the years. Twenty-four years of soldiering. Twenty-five if I counted that part-time bit in the State Guard. It all began during World War II; 1944 was the year and a new recruit was paid fifty dollars a month. I was seventeen years old, five-foot-five, and 145 pounds of enthusiasm.

The Marine Corps turned me down!

Dejected, I tried them all and received the same reply, "Sorry."

Poor eyesight and a history of tuberculosis as a kid just did not help a guy at all. I was walking in downtown Los Angeles when I happened to see the sign, "American Seamen For American Ships – Join the US Maritime Service." That was my ticket to the war.

We marched through the city on our way from the recruiting station to the train depot. Our journey had started. I remember how people looked and sometimes waved as we marched by. We felt like "heroes" off to war.

"Hit the deck and move out!" Suddenly we found out how the road to war would be paved. Still, we were young and eager. "Damn the submarines, we're the men of the Merchant Marine!"

When I was eighteen I volunteered for the Army. I could not enlist but they would accept me through the Selective Service System. I was assigned to an infantry unit as a machine gunner. However, the war ended before I could get any machine gun into action, so it was to Japan for occupation duty. But I can still hear the call, "Machine guns up!" And I would run forward with thirty-five pounds of MG barrel across my shoulders and my pack digging into my back.

"The Corps has been good to me," I thought. "The only outfit for a professional soldier." I joined the Corps in 1952 after I returned from Korea. That war was still going on and the Corps no longer cared about my eyesight or that I had TB as a kid. Squad Leader and Platoon Sergeant. Jaunal's Raiders and the General's wife. That was a story! Gunnery Sergeant of a one-five-five gun battery. How many landings? My first Company as a First Sergeant was Company C, First Anti-Tank Battalion. This was my last Company, Heat and Steam of Third Amtracs.

I took my place with the Battalion staff. The Battalion was ready. The Sergeant Major called the Battalion to attention as the Commanding Officer, Lieutenant Colonel Robert E. Haebel (Media, Pennsylvania), approached.

The Sergeant Major ordered me forward. "First Sergeant Jaunal, front and center."

I marched forward and reported to the Colonel.

"It is very seldom we get to promote a man to the top rung of the ladder in this Battalion. It gives me great pleasure to present to you this warrant." The Colonel then began to read my warrant, "To all who shall see these presents, greeting, know ye that reposing special trust and confidence in the fidelity and abilities of Jack W. Jaunal, I do appoint him a Sergeant Major in the United States Marine Corps."

As the Colonel continued to read my warrant I could feel the pride and prestige of the title, "Sergeant Major," flow through my veins. Another phase of my military career had ended and a new one was about to begin.

"Signed by Leonard F. Chapman, Commandant of the Marine Corps."

The Colonel looked me in the eye, smiled and said, "Congratulations, SERGEANT MAJOR."

9 April 1968

My gear was in the jeep. I climbed aboard and told my driver to "shove off." I was on my way. It had been thirteen years since I left Recon. I was looking forward to this assignment. Recon had grown in size over the years, from a company to a battalion.

I waved to the guard as we drove out the gate. "Third Amtracs is a good outfit," I thought. But I had always wanted to return to Recon and now I was on my way. Last time I was a Staff Sergeant in a Division Recon Company; now I would be Sergeant Major of a Recon Battalion.

I remember the old Company, Japan in 1954, the Third Marine Division. When the Company Gunny yelled, "Fall in," you could hear one hundred and twenty heels go "click."

Our Recon chant could be heard all over the countryside during our five mile runs. "Up the hill, down the hill, RECON, all the way."

Cocky and high spirited, we figured ourselves a cut above the other Marines in the division. We had fifty mile hikes before President Kennedy made them popular. And the climb up Mount Fuji, now that was a hike! Helicopters, rubber boats, submarines, jeeps, and feet. We used them all. After that came parachutes and scuba gear.

The sign along the road read:

> First Reconnaissance Battalion,
> First Marine Division, FMF
> LtCol B.C. Stinemetz.

Chris parked the jeep in front of Battalion Headquarters. As I got out of the jeep I noticed an officer approaching.

"Can I help you?" he said.

"I'm reporting aboard, Sir." I noticed he was a Lieutenant Colonel.

"I'm Colonel Stinemetz. Welcome aboard Sergeant Major."

Nothing like being met by the old man himself. The Colonel pointed me toward the Battalion Headquarters area and said he would talk to me later. He was on his way to Division Headquarters.

It was time to send Chris back to Amtracs. For me it was just another cruise. For him, another month over here and then home to his wife and daughter in Idaho. You seldom say goodbye in the Corps, just a "So long" will do. There was not much to say – just a feeling of comradeship.

"So long Chris, take care of yourself."

We shook hands.

"I'll try to see you before I go home, Sergeant Major."

I watched as he drove off and knew he probably would not get a chance to be here again.

I picked up my gear and walked toward my new hooch. It felt good to be back in Recon, especially as a Sergeant Major.

10 April 1968

The Recon Marine sometimes likes to think of himself as a special breed of Marine, the elite of an elite Corps. He is what makes the Army's beret turn green with envy. He is airborne, scuba-trained, and ranger schooled in survival.

The water buffalo in Vietnam is an unpredictable creature with a bad temper when he decides to be. He may leave you alone when you are trying to attract his attention, or he may attack for no reason at all.

The four-man Recon patrol was crossing one of the Vietnamese fields when they came upon a herd of water buffalo. For no reason, one of the buffalos decided to charge the last Marine of the patrol as he crossed the buffalo trail. As the ugly-natured animal chased the Marine around in circles, his buddies stood back and roared with laughter. Suddenly their merriment ceased as they noticed another buffalo joining the charge. Unable to get away, they opened fire. At the same time, the first buffalo decided to stop playing and charge his Marine. Head down and moving like a Sherman tank, the animal ran directly toward the Marine.

At that moment, this combat-ready warrior — jungle suit, commando hat, airborne wings on his chest, ammunition belt slung about his body, and knife in his boot — fired his weapon at the attacking enemy. On came the buffalo, right over the top of the Marine. As he went down, his legs came up, and he shot himself in the toe!

His buddies, meantime, had scattered the herd and came running to his rescue. As they picked him up, the wounded warrior asked, "Did you see the sniper that got me?"

23 April 1968

"Come in," I said, holding open the door of my hut as the Company mail clerk carried in two large packages.

"Sergeant Major, I bet you get more mail than anyone else in this Battalion," he said as he put the packages on a wooden bench near my field desk. He handed me several letters and said, "And most of it from women."

"I guess that's the advantage of being a Camp Fire Girl or a drill team adviser," I replied.

As the clerk left I looked at the return address to see who sent the packages. Most of the packages would be from the Camp Fire groups in Seattle, most of the letters from the drill team.

During my tour of duty as a Marine recruiter in Seattle, I became a drill team adviser to the Kent-Meridian High School "Royalettes" Girls Drill Team and several members of that team wrote to me each week. The packages were from Mrs. Harold D. Hardin of the O-Ki-Hi Camp Fire Girl Group – that was my outfit.

I had been an honorary member of the O-Ki-Hi Group for a few years now. To the best of my knowledge I was the only known Marine Camp Fire Girl in Vietnam. I had my new membership card, sent by the group, with my current address listed as Vietnam.

Because I was a member of the O-Ki-Hi Group they decided one of their projects would be to supply me with "goodies" packages to be given out to the Marines in my

Battalion. And so every few weeks some packages would arrive in the mail for me to deliver to Marines.

Inside the packages would be pocket novels, writing paper, envelopes, and other items, like toothpaste. But most of the contents were cookies and cakes – hence the "goodies" package.

Most of the time I gave the packages to patrols returning from the bush or observation post (OP) duty. Those homemade cakes and cookies tasted better after a week or so of field rations. And the time I received the chocolate-covered Camp Fire Girl mints – devoured in seconds!

It was time to write to Mrs. Hardin:

Received your letter, photos, and two large packages today. Thank you very much. I will see that they are delivered to my Marines.

As you notice I am no longer in the Amphibian Tractor Battalion. I received my promotion to Sergeant Major and am now Sergeant Major of the First Reconnaissance Battalion. Our mission is to scout and observe enemy activity. Our patrols stay out in the "bush" for about six days, return and then go out again in four or five days.

When I think of the first time I met your group of girls, and compare it with your recent photo, I find it almost unbelievable that they are such young ladies now. I shall keep one photo displayed in my office so others can see my "outfit."

The reconnaissance patrol "Rice Krispies" from Company A was selected as the squad to receive the "goodies."

This reconnaissance patrol recently returned from an observation post deep within enemy territory, where it had been for 11 days observing

*enemy activity, and calling in artillery fire on Viet
Cong and North Vietnamese Army troops.*

*According to their First Sergeant they are the
most decorated patrol in the Battalion. Previous
members have been recommended for all awards
up to the Medal of Honor.*

End of letter. We Camp Fire Girls do have our various
responsibilities.

❁

26 April 1968

It was early morning and the Colonel and I were on our way to the First Hospital Company, about one half mile down the road from our Battalion area.

One of our reconnaissance patrols by the name of "Rice Krispies" had been hit about four o'clock in the morning by enemy mortar or rocket fire. Their mission was completed and they were to be lifted out by helicopter at daylight. Seven enemy rounds hit them – the first one hit a rock directly in their position. One Marine was killed, the radio operator; three were wounded, one seriously.

We arrived at the hospital just as the Medevac helicopter arrived. As it landed, a couple of corpsmen ran out with a stretcher. It was the KIA, the body wrapped in a rain poncho. We followed them into the receiving hut. The corpsman cut the binding and unwrapped the poncho. It was a young Marine, probably no more than nineteen. He was covered with dirt and blood, and although he had been on patrol for five days he had very few whiskers. Too young to grow a beard yet. He was hit in the back by shrapnel, going through his pack and radio. The back of his head was bloody. "Looks as if it was the one in the back of the head that killed him."

I noticed the dead Marine's First Sergeant had entered. He is a short man, tough and all Marine Corps. I sometimes think of him as a small bulldog. A fighter. I noticed the "Bulldog's" eyes, they looked a little misty. He came down to identify the body, one of the more unpleasant tasks of a First Sergeant; it hurts the good ones especially. "He was a good man." I remembered seeing the Marine in the area; he looked different then. It was the Rice Krispies patrol that recently received two boxes of cookies from the O-Ki-Hi Camp Fire Girls in Seattle.

The corpsman took off the dead Marine's identification tag. The body was pale, eyes open. It had been about five hours since he was hit. It is a little hard to take every time you see one of these wounded or dead Marines. It must be a fatherly reaction or maybe I subconsciously think of my own sons.

As they removed articles from the body, I noticed a small piece of cloth, about three by five inches. It was red and white with a small patch of blue in one corner. Dirty, with some of his blood on it, it was between his chest and camouflage jacket. A small US flag. "He was a good Marine." And he thought enough of his flag to carry it on patrol with him. As it was taken from his young and now lifeless body I could not help but think of other young men, alive, who burn or try to burn our flag – the flag this young Marine died for.

I am in no mood for flag burners today.

❀

28 April 1968

It was in the winter of 1944-45 when I met one of my first wartime amputees. I was on my way to the West Coast on a military flight that was grounded at Ogden, Utah, because of bad weather conditions.

The next morning there were quite a few of us waiting for a hop out. We gathered at flight operations and I was talking to a soldier, not much older than I was. He was on his way home from the hospital, convalescent leave. His left foot was gone at the ankle.

"No flight today," announced flight operations. We all gave a little groan. "Socked in all over the West."

There would be another day of waiting. We put on our coats and started back to the transient barracks. I walked along with my new companion. There were about two inches of snow on the ground. As we walked along I noticed the trail we left. There were two small holes in the snow from my companion's crutches, and only one foot print. Three foot prints in the snow.

I was thinking about those snow tracks as I waited to see one of our Recon Marines at the Navy hospital near Da Nang. The Marine had recently been wounded on patrol. His right leg had to be amputated at the hip. The doctor was having a fresh bandage put on. It was shrapnel that tore the Marine's leg apart. He was a young Marine, nineteen, class of sixty-seven at his high school in New York. They seem younger now, but they are not. It is just that World War II was many years ago.

The first question the Marine asked when he was brought back to the ward was, "Will I have to get out of the Marine Corps?" He didn't know if he wanted to make a career of it but "I hoped to be around a little while yet." I told him about a one-legged Marine Gunny Sergeant still in the Corps. He perked up a bit at the thought of staying in. He had been a Marine less than a year – recruit training at Parris Island, and Army Airborne School followed by his assignment to the First Reconnaissance Battalion in Vietnam.

The Assistant Commandant of the Marine Corps, Lieutenant General Lew Walt, was in the area and had visited the hospital ward. While visiting, General Walt had presented him the Purple Heart Medal. He was sure proud of that Medal. "He sat here for about fifteen minutes talking to me," said the Marine. He showed me the medal. "I always wanted one," he said, "but I didn't think I would get it this way."

His career in the Marine Corps was over, but he will be a Marine the rest of his life.

As I left the hospital I remembered those snow tracks in forty-five, and wondered if there would be snow on the ground when that young Marine returned to his home in New York.

12 May 1968

Today I went back to my old outfit, Third Amtracs, for a visit. I wanted to see the formal dedication of the camp in memory of the Marine it was named for.

The camp was dedicated in the memory of Corporal Charles R. Lauer (Downey, California), an Amphibian Tractor Crew Chief in Company A.

On 18 June 1967, Corporal Lauer and his crew were crossing a river under heavy enemy machine gun fire to rescue a wounded Marine. After the first rescue he spotted another wounded Marine and performed his second rescue.

There was a third wounded Marine to rescue. The enemy had Lauer's LVT in a deadly crossfire. Manning his .30 caliber machine gun as his vehicle drove toward the wounded Marine, Lauer knocked out the enemy emplacement. While doing so, Lauer himself was killed.

Lauer's actions saved the lives of three wounded Marines and the aggressive employment of his LVT provided protection for many others. For his gallantry in action, Corporal Lauer was posthumously awarded the Navy Cross.

Following the ceremony, the Battalion mess hall, built by the 128th Construction Battalion (Seabees), USN*, was dedicated and named for Petty Officer Third Class Keith A. McEnamy. Petty Officer McEnamy was killed by an enemy mine 24 September 1967.

* See Glossary

17 May 1968*

Patrol hit by lightning last night; one man died in hospital.

One man wounded by enemy booby trap.

Went to see Ginny Anderson at Da Nang Press Club; she wants to do story about Recon for *Highline Times.*

19 May 1968*

Ho Chi Minh birthday!

20 May 1968*

Flew on resupply mission to Ba Na and Dong Den.

22 May 1968*

One KIA reported and two WIA.

SSgt Hughes killed with First Air Cav – he told me it would happen and he was right.

*From my Journal. JWJ

24 May 1968*

Major Keating, our S-3 officer, died of wounds.
Our observers were with teams from the Air Cav to view their methods of operation in the Que Son area and A Shau valley. An exchange of tactical ideas, especially Recon inserts.

26 May 1968*

Memorial services for Major Keating and SSgt Hughes.
Darn near cried. (Both had been assigned to temporary duty with the First Cavalry during the A Shau Valley campaign.)

28 May 1968*

Team in trouble, one KIA, four fell off cliff.
1700 went to NSA Hosp to see WIAs brought in.
The Recon Marines reported they had been attacked by an enemy force and had been forced to leave their position to take cover on a jungle cliff. An intensive search by Marine helicopters located part of the Recon team under the jungle canopy.

*From my Journal. JWJ

29 May 1968*

Tried to go out with rescue team.
Rest of team brought in 1230.
Went to visit at First Hospital Company.

30 May 1968*

Went out to Hill 10 and back.
Patrol ran into trouble, one KIA and one WIA.

31 May 1968*

Two patrols in trouble – four WIAs.

*From my Journal. JWJ

31 May 1968*

A running gun battle between eight reconnaissance Marines and eighty North Vietnamese Army (NVA) soldiers left a trail of communist bodies as the enemy unsuccessfully attempted to cut off the Leathernecks' route to safety.

The 45-minute gun fight started moments after a 1st Force Reconnaissance Company team was inserted on a reconnaissance mission atop a hill south of Phu Bai.

Sergeant Robert F. Buda (1425 E. Ocotillo, Phoenix, Arizona), who single-handedly killed 15 of the enemy, said his team was immediately surrounded by NVA after the enemy discovered their position.

The 1st Division Marines quickly moved down the hill, but were chased by more NVA. As the downhill race continued, the NVA attempted to outflank the Marines on both sides.

At the foot of the hill, the Recon Marines formed a perimeter and took stock of the situation.

"We heard movement all around us," said Buda. "They had us completely surrounded."

In the evening darkness an enemy soldier managed to crawl to within 15 feet of the Marines. Buda saw him first and killed him before the NVA could fire a shot.

From the top of the hill, grenades were thrown at the Marines. "With the grenades and all the movement around us, we figured we had better fight our way back to the top of the hill," recalled Buda.

The eight Leathernecks regrouped and headed for the top of the hill. The NVA closed in, but three were killed when they were spotted in the thick brush.

The communists figured out what the Marines were trying to do and attempted to close in, but the thick jungle brush prevented them from moving quickly. Each side could hear the other shouting commands.

It became evident that whoever controlled the top of the hill would have the advantage. A desperate race began between the Marines and NVA.

The Marines won, but only by yards. The NVA were right behind the recon patrol when it reached the top.

*News report in *Sea Tiger* by Sergeant Dave Martinez

When Buda spotted 15 communists 25 yards away he quickly set up a claymore mine he was carrying and hid behind a tree. Seconds later, as the NVA charged up the trail, Buda detonated the claymore.

The confusion that followed allowed the Marines time to call for an extraction helicopter. Minutes later, a CH-46* "Sea Knight" hovered over the recon team.

Because it was impossible for the aircraft to land in the rugged terrain, the Marines were hauled up by a hoist, one man at a time. As each Marine rose through the air, the enemy concentrated heavy small arms fire on him.

* See Glossary

24 June 1968

Ba Na is a former French resort atop a mountain 1,460 meters high, twelve miles west of Da Nang and a few miles south. During its prime Ba Na was probably one of the elite resorts of old Indochina. Now it is in ruins from the ravages of time, nature, and war. The top of the mountain is not very large, maybe 100 meters long and thirty meters wide. The sides are cliffs that go straight down for thirty meters or more. The ends of the ridge go out and down to connect with the other ridges or fingers in the terrain.

It can be warm and sunny on Ba Na, and sometimes you are in the clouds or above them. At night it can be chilly – from a cool breeze to teeth-chattering cold.

Ba Na is one of our Battalion OPs and a radio relay station. The primary mission is radio relay. The radio station can maintain contact with the Battalion CP and all our patrols operating in the field. It has been a life saver on more than one occasion.

We send about twenty Marines to Ba Na for ten days at a time to provide security. Two Marines operate the radio station.

I was with a patrol from Company E, called "Slate Creek." The patrol leader was Staff Sergeant Marroquin, better known to many Marines as "The Mad Mexican." While on Ba Na I would check defensive positions, bunkers, barbed wire, and living conditions in general.

It was seven in the morning when we landed on Ba Na. There is only one way in, or out, and that is by helicopter. It would be Monday, two days later, before the chopper would be back.

The Mad Mexican was preparing to send out a five man Recon patrol to check the trails on one side of the mountain. I decided to go along as "an extra gun."

We crawled through our defensive barbed wire and hardly got started when the last Marine in the patrol accidentally set off one of our trip flares.

Slowly we made our way along an old trail and through the bush. When we came to the top of the first ridge, I checked the area with binoculars.

"Can't see anything but canopy or jungle."

We continued down toward a flat area and then blazed our own trail down between two ridges. The brush was thick, and you could lose sight of the Marine ten feet ahead of you. Overhead you could not see the sky. The point man was using his knife to help cut the trail. It was hot in there. Perspiration made my uniform damp. Vegetation wrapped around my arms and legs.

We came into a clearing on a small ledge about twelve feet above an old house. Only walls of the house remained and the jungle was taking possession. We had to jump to the ground below.

I was the fourth man to go – only I went sooner than anticipated. A piece of the ledge gave way and I fell to the ground below. My right foot hit the ground, the edge of a stream bed, the rest of me kept going. My fall was softened by the bushes I landed on. I was in a small, dry stream bed. My feet were up, my head down – a tangled mess of grenades and equipment. I crawled up, mad at myself for messing up the patrol.

Hurts. Hurts. Like smarts.

"Is it broken, Sir?" a Marine whispered. We always seem to whisper. And if Charlie (VC) didn't hear my fall, he must be deaf or not in the immediate area. "I don't know," I replied.

I was still able to walk, more or less. "Let's move out," I told the Patrol Leader. Oh, how it hurt.

"Want me to carry any of your gear?" asked a Marine. "No thanks," I replied.

We continued through more jungle. My foot went from numb-hurt to hurt-hurt. Out of the jungle and into a large clearing. The clearing is part of an old road. At one time there must have been a road to the top of Ba Na. The map we had only indicated a trail. Looking up we could see the top of Ba Na.

"Keep moving," said the Patrol Leader.

We entered under the jungle canopy again and continued downward on a narrow trail. After we crossed a small stream bed, the radio operator said, "Wait." We stopped, poised for action.

My foot was throbbing with pain. I was dirty, scratched, and wet from perspiration. The radio operator turned around, looked at me and said, "I want to take your picture." I did not know whether to be pleased or angry. "Click." Everyone has a camera!

We moved on, another ruins to check. There are several ruins of what we call the old French cabana – resort living of days long past. Upward. Hurt. We checked two more ruins in a small cleared area. Off the trail and up to more ruins. The radio operator gently gave me a shove as I crawled up a six-foot embankment.

We climbed along one of the trails back to the top. The pain was becoming greater every time we stopped; it hurt to start walking again. Then it was almost straight up to the top of Ba Na. I grabbed a tree stump and pulled myself up a step. Stump, sweat, step, and more pain. And more pain.

It went that way to the barbed wire, half way up. Cleared the wire, then up. Hands in dirt, crawl, one step at a time. Six feet to go, straight up, nothing to grip, no holds, and then strong arms reached out, "Grab hold, Sergeant Major," and a Marine pulled me over the top of Ba Na.

"A beautiful view."

When I took my boot off, my ankle looked like a large grapefruit. A Marine bandaged my foot; he did a good job. We had no corpsman with us. Our Navy corpsmen are excellent, only there are not enough of them in our Battalion.

Another patrol went out. They found some traces of VC only a few days old. That night something set off two of our flares. The Mad Mexican called for artillery fire on the ridge line 200 meters out. We had a quiet night except for some rats in the area.

Monday morning. The resupply bird would be up. I finished my breakfast of C-rations, gathered my gear, ready to leave. The bird arrived and I hobbled aboard.

I even walked, more or less, to the X-ray room at the hospital. I was examined. A corpsman brought me a pair of crutches.

"What are these for?" I asked.

"For you," the corpsman replied. "The doctor says you have a fractured ankle."

28 June 1968*

Brought back American flag from Ba Na OP – flag sent to me by American Legion Post #134, Burien, Washington. Will return to 134 when I return to the "World." While waiting for helo-lift back to Battalion, had flag taken down from building. The Mad Mexican sent two Marines to "take down the Colors for the Sergeant Major."

"Do you know how to do it?" asked the Mad Mexican.

"Yes, Sir," replied the two Marines, "by the book."

Although I could not see the ceremony, I could hear the commands and the Marines conduct a formal color guard ceremony. Brings forth the pride. Later, the Mad Mexican returned, "Here's your flag, Sergeant Major, all done-up regulation."

There is something about Marines and the Flag ...

*From my Journal. JWJ

29 June 1968

The Colonel and I stood at the top of the small hill that overlooks the LZ (landing zone). From the LZ to the top of the hill is about one hundred meters. Our Recon patrols claim it is the hardest climb in Vietnam. At the top is "home," our Battalion area.

One of our Recon patrols from Company A was found by Charlie and a Marine was killed. We sent for choppers to bring them out.

"It's like *Twelve O'Clock High*, only different."

"What did you say, Sergeant Major?"

"I said it is like *Twelve O'Clock High*, Sir."

"What do you mean?"

"Reminds me of the World War II movie about bombing raids and how the ground crews sweat it out."

"I see what you mean."

Every morning at daybreak our patrols begin to go down to the LZ. Dressed in their camouflage uniforms, faces painted, loaded down with weapons, ammo, and field rations for five days. The birds (helicopters) come in, the patrols go aboard, and it is out to the bush for four days.

We watch them go. We wait. When they are in trouble, we crowd around the radio in the operations center and listen. We "sweat it out." And we watch them return.

In *Twelve O'Clock High*, it's early in the morning and the bomber crews head for the flight line. Pilots and crew board their aircraft. As each plane takes off, those left behind begin to sweat it out. If the flight runs into trouble, everyone crowds around the operations radio and listens. Eyes dart skyward as the first sound of the engines is heard. "There they are!" The bombers come in – one, two, three – the count begins. As the planes land, the ground crews rush out to meet them. Buddies help each other along. Another mission completed. Gregory Peck can relax.

I hear a Marine say, "There they are!"

The helicopters are coming in with our Recon patrol. As the helicopters come in to land, Marines from Company A, and others, start down the hill to greet them. The birds land, the tail gate drops, and a dirty, tired Recon patrol comes out.

The count begins – one, two, three –

"One KIA."

As the Marines start to walk up the hill, buddies greet each other. You see one Marine helping another with his gear, helping to ease the load. There are questions and answers.

"They were all around us."

"I was glad to see those birds."

As the Marines file by, the Colonel and I greet them. Another patrol in. We can relax.

"Yes, Sir, sort of like *Twelve O'Clock High*."

29 June 1968*

Two KIAs and one WIA from Company A.
Leg sore from walking on cast – one week ago today fractured leg.

3 July 1968*

Lost eight men, went down in copter shot down. All lost (thirteen total).

4 July 1968*

Lieutenant wounded in head today while on patrol.

5 July 1968*

Visited patients at NSA Hospital.

*From my Journal. JWJ

✿

7 July 1968

It is like the rest of the huts, only a little larger and painted white. A small red Torii stands in front, a ship's bell hangs from the top of it, and a sign reads "Chapel On The Hill." It overlooks our landing zone. Helicopters have a habit of drowning out part of the church services.

The chapel was almost full when I entered. It would be crowded today, with Marines outside listening before the memorial was over.

It was a rough one to take. Eight men lost, all at one time. Our largest single loss to date. One of our Recon patrols was being inserted when their helicopter came under enemy fire. The helicopter had almost landed when Charlie opened up. The pilot radioed "under fire," tried to take off, and as he did so the chopper was hit. The report from the escort aircraft said it "went up in a ball of flame," fell to the ground and exploded. The pilot, co-pilot, two crewmen and our eight men were killed. Our Reaction Force went in and brought out the bodies. The only man not burned was the pilot. He had been blown out of the aircraft.

I looked at the Memorial program. They were listed by faith.

Latter Day Saints.
Private First Class . . . US Marine Corps

Catholic.
> Sergeant . . . US Marine Corps. He had just reenlisted the day before.
> Corporal . . . US Marine Corps.
> Lance Corporal . . . US Marine Corps.

Protestant.
> Captain . . . US Marine Corps. In country five days, on his second tour of duty in Vietnam. Went along to observe the insert.
> Corporal . . . US Marine Corps.
> Lance Corporal . . . US Marine Corps.

Jewish.
> Corpsman . . . US Navy.

Normally we only have one Chaplain; today there were four. It was time to begin. The Chaplain of the Church of Latter Day Saints began the service.

We prayed. "Our Father – "

The Catholic Chaplain read the scriptures. We sang a hymn. The Protestant Chaplain gave the sermon, a memorial. We listened – and remembered.

The Jewish Chaplain gave a prayer.

We sang.

> *"Eternal Father, grant we pray,*
> *To all Marines,* (always stronger here) *both night and day*
> *The courage, honor, strength and skill*
> *Their land to serve, Thy law fulfill;*
> *Be Thou the shield* (loud and strong again) *forever more*
> *From ev'ry peril to the Corps."*

Bodies straightened as they sang and the words became stronger at the end. As the hymn faded away, everyone came to attention as they heard the firing squad.

"Ready, aim, fire!" "CRACK"

"Ready, aim, fire!" "CRACK"

As the saluting volley was fired I noticed a young Sergeant in front of me; his shoulders twitched with every crack of the rifles.

"Ready, aim, fire!" "CRACK"

And then the sound of Taps flowed through the air, through the chapel on the hill and across the fields. There is no sound more fitting for the military than Taps, sad and yet beautiful. It can make the tears flow. There had been a tear or two in the eyes of those in the chapel. It is hard to keep that small wet trail off the cheek. I know.

8 July 1968

"We were in an ambush site in Phu Loc Valley," stated Sergeant John A. Sleeper (South Lancaster, Massachusetts), a patrol leader from our Company C, "when a company of NVA – about 100 – came strolling down the trail as though they owned the countryside. The four-man-point element wasn't even looking around. They wore utilities. Some had helmets, and they were well armed. We saw .50 caliber machine guns, rockets and rocket launchers."

According to Sleeper, twenty-three NVA soldiers passed his ambush position before he detonated the claymore mines and the Marines opened fire. "I decided that it was better to hit in front of the column before one of the enemy spotted our position."

The surprise of the ambush, a heavy volume of rifle fire and over thirty hand grenades accounted for thirty-five enemy dead. The Recon Marines then escaped through a gap left in the enemy lines by two NVA dead.

"We called in artillery and close air support," Sleeper said. "They did a fantastic job, hitting the enemy with pinpoint accuracy."

Sergeant Sleeper consolidated his team of thirteen Marines on a knoll and set up a 360 degree perimeter defense. "The enemy followed us and probed the knoll with small arms and hand grenades," he said. "I radioed for an extraction and a helicopter picked us up." There were no Marine casualties.

Sergeant Sleeper was awarded the Silver Star Medal for his leadership during the action. He had also been awarded the Bronze Star Medal for a previous Recon patrol action.

14 July 1968*

Attended church services for two KIAs.

15 July 1968*

Two men lost on patrol – got separated.

18 July 1968*

Put a sign up on the LZ named in honor of Major Keating – "Keating Field" – unofficial but who will know the difference?

26 July 1968*

Tried to get cast off early but Doc said "not yet" – 10 more days.

Change of command – LtCol Stinemetz out, LtCol Charon in.

*From my Journal. JWJ

26 July 1968*

After nine days of orientation and training, 21 Leathernecks of the 1st Reconnaissance Bn., 1st Marine Division, completed the battalion's reconnaissance indoctrination program (RIP).

The nine-day course, geared for Marines joining the recon unit for the first time, included communications procedures, first aid, civic action and the M-16 rifle. The men also attended a three day Land Mine Warfare course.

"This concept is designed to give our new men an insight into what recon is and what we do," explained SgtMaj. Jack Jaunal, (1250 S. 159th St., Seattle, Wash.). "By successfully completing these nine days of training, they should have no problem at all in the field."

LtCol. B.C. Stinemetz, commanding officer of the battalion, presented diplomas to the men.

* News item in *Sea Tiger* by Lance Corporal Steve Wyatt

28 July 1968*

0700 – Had scare. H-53 exploded in air, thought 25 of our Recon Marines on board. Was wrong chopper – all hands lost.

29 July 1968*

Recon team "shot out" of landing zone.

30 July 1968*

KIA last night was Marine who took my photo on Ba Na patrol.

1 August 1968*

OP on Hill 200 overrun by NVA – 11 WIA.
5 KIA – Reaction Force Company E –
3 WIA by boobytrap.
Patrol hit, one KIA.

*From my Journal. JWJ

2 August 1968

The following letter was written by Marine Lance Corporal Donald E. Griss, Company A, Fifth Shore Party Battalion, and printed in the *Sea Tiger.*

Just imagine, most of the guys over here are 18 and fighting to make it 19. The average age of the combat soldier in many units here is 18½. And what a man he is, a pink-cheeked, tousle-haired, tight muscled fellow who under normal circumstances would be considered by society as half man and half boy, not yet dry behind the ears and a pain in the unemployment chart. But here and now, he is the beardless hope of free man.

He is, for the most part, unmarried and without material possessions except possibly for an old car at home and a transistor radio here. He listens to rock-'n-roll and 105 millimeter howitzers.

He's just out of school, received so-so grades, played a little football, and had a girl who promised to be true. He has learned to drink beer, because it is cold and 'is the thing to do.' He is a Private First Class, a none-year veteran with one or possibly three years to go. He never cared for work, preferred waxing his own car to washing his father's, but he is now working or fighting from dawn to dark, often longer.

He can dig a foxhole, apply first aid to a wounded companion, march until he is told to stop or stop until he is told to march. He has stood among hills of bodies, and he has helped to build those hills. He has wept in private and in public, and has not been ashamed of doing either, because his pals have fallen in battle and he has come close to joining them.

He has become self-sufficient. He has two pairs of fatigues, washes one and wears the other. He sometimes forgets to brush his teeth, but not his rifle. He keeps his socks dry and his canteen full. He can cook his own meals, fix his rips – material or mental.

He will share his water with you if you are thirsty, break his rations in half if you are hungry, and split his ammunition if you are fighting for your life. He can do the work of two civilians, draw half the pay of one, and yet find ironic humor in it all.

He has learned to use his hands as a weapon, and his weapon as his hands. He can save a life or most assuredly take one. He is now 19, a veteran, and fighting to make it 20. What a man!

2 August 1968*

Took Navy chamber pressure test for Scuba – simulated 105-foot dive & leveled off at 60 feet – 30 minutes breathing pure oxygen.
Colonel flew to Phu Bai.

5 August 1968*

Removed cast from leg.   Feels good, ankle weak, not walking real good yet.

6 August 1968*

Accidental discharge .45 on Hill 200 – Medevac man with tip of little toe shot off.

7 August 1968*

1830 – Went to First Hospital Company. Three Marines from Hill 425 brought in. Injured from .50 MG exploding, all OK.

---

*From my Journal. JWJ

*11 August 1968**

One KIA and one WIA, from our own claymore, accident on Hill 425 (Company B).

*14 August 1968**

1400 – Patrol from Company E captured three NVA or VC.
1500 – Memorial service for KIA.

*21 August 1968**

Patrol from Company E found enemy camp. Killed three NVA – a girl, probably a nurse, got away. Brought in eleven enemy rifles and automatic weapons.
Alert tonight.
Practice forming of a provisional infantry battalion.

*22 August 1968**

Hill 200 hit, one KIA and three WIAs; Company E Reaction Force in at 0600. Visited wounded in hospital.
Rappelled out of helicopter with Company A. Surprised hell out of First Sgt.

*From my Journal. JWJ

22 August 1968

About eighteen miles southwest of Da Nang, on a hill overlooking the Song Vu Gia River, is one of our Combat OPs. It is Hill 200, an OP that has obtained many good sightings on enemy activities in the valley below.

Recently Charlie lost 178 men after the Recon Marines on Hill 200 called in artillery fire and air strikes on some of their sightings. Charlie would like Recon out of his area of operations.

He tried to take the hill the first of August. It was early in the morning when he hit, a few hours before daylight. Using AT rockets, hand grenades, bangalore torpedoes and small arms fire, Charlie overran the position. Once inside he placed charges alongside bunkers – "He's inside the wire!" A wounded Marine, Corporal Roger P. Keister (Phoenix, Arizona), the senior man alive, realizing that the position was becoming untenable, ordered the remaining Marines down the southern slope of the hill. When he observed Charlie starting to withdraw from the position, he rallied his remaining Marines, all wounded, and rushed back up the hill, killing three of the enemy himself. We lost five Marines.

By early morning the Reaction Force from the Battalion landed by helicopter and regained possession of the Hill. Before leaving, Charlie managed to place his flag over one of the bunkers and it greeted the Marines as they landed. Since that day the US flag has flown over Hill 200 twenty-four hours a day.

Charlie tried to take the hill again on August twenty-first. He got only as far as the barbed wire entanglements. The battle lasted nine and one-half hours, the longest single engagement for the Recon Marines. During the night the flag was brought down twice by the enemy's fire. And twice it was raised by the Staff Sergeant in command of the OP. He exposed himself twice to enemy fire to raise the flag, once after he was wounded. Later he was killed during the battle.

The flag was brought back to his company, Company E, to hang in his honor.

When an American Legion post requested a "Battle-worn US flag from Vietnam" for their Veteran's Day Parade in November, they wrote to me. I asked Company E about the Hill 200 flag.

The original owner of the Hill 200 flag, Lance Corporal Marvin D. Schlicher (Bera, Ohio), volunteered to donate his flag from Hill 200. The flag now belongs in the Sergeant James J. Bealin Post of the American Legion, Brooklyn, New York.

Corporal Keister received the Silver Star Medal for his actions on Hill 200 and a Meritorious Combat promotion to Sergeant.

23 August 1968*

0350 – Alert.
0500 – Secured.
0600 – Two rockets hit hill behind us.
0630 – Company A (ProvInfCo) preparing to mount out. Rocket hit near guard bunker #4 in paddy. Company A to Cam Le Bridge to support MPs.

The next day, as we entered the outskirts of the village, we passed some mortar positions. The village, called Hoa Vang, is less than two miles south of the Da Nang Air Base. This was the second day of the battle at the Cam Le Bridge on the south end of the village. The fighting would last for three days.

The Cam Le Bridge, 500 meters long, crosses the Song Cau Do River. The south end had an old French bunker; the north end is Hoa Vang village. The bunker was destroyed; the village survived.

The VC and NVA forces tried to take the bridge by infiltrating Hoa Vang. They lost about 200 men. We passed more than a few dead bodies as we drove through. The marketplace was pretty well burned out. Last time I was here, my driver stopped to buy some bananas from a vendor.

During the fighting, a Marine fire truck from the air wing tried to save the buildings while fighting was going on. Two of the Marines assigned to protect the firefighters were wounded by sniper fire.

*From my Journal. JWJ

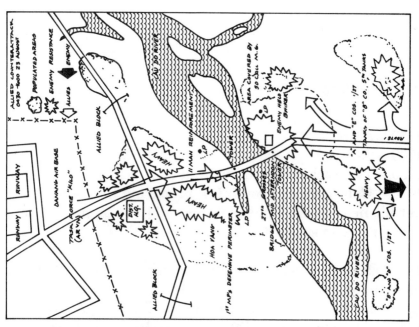

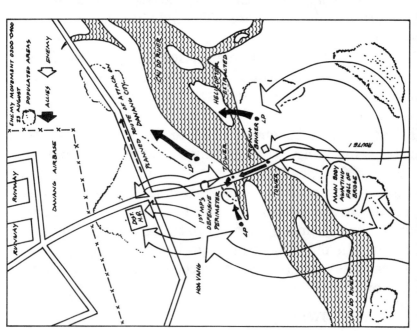

Battle of Cam Le Bridge. Enemy movement (*left map*); Allied counterattack (*right map*), 23 August 1968.
(Based on sketches from the *Marine Corps GAZETTE*, February 1970.)

"Zing, crack, rat-a-tat-tat!"

The firing grew louder as we pulled up to the bridge. I went to a small building off to the right. It was the CP for Company A of our Battalion.

Our Battalion formed a provisional infantry company to serve as a reserve force for the Division during this latest offensive by Charlie. Because our primary mission is reconnaissance, our companies are smaller than the infantry ones. Also, because we had many patrols in the bush, Company A was brought up to infantry size by additional Marines from Company B and Headquarters Company.

The Recon Marines were fighting as "grunts" and doing a fine job of it. At first, they had been used as a blocking force, and now they held positions from the bridge, to the right, along the river and from the river north through the outskirts of Hoa Vang, to the main road – Highway One.

Cam Le Bridge on Highway One leads directly to the Da Nang Air Base. Charlie wanted the bridge for access to Da Nang City and for the air base.

I located the Company First Sergeant.

"We're stacking 'em up on the other end of the bridge. Had their flag up for a little while but we blew it away," said the First Sergeant. The Company A First Sergeant was Otis Barker (Baltimore, Maryland), a small, tough veteran of three wars and one of the best "Firsts" in the Corps. "Charlie held one end of the bridge for a little while, but we've cleared it now."

When the VC and NVA forces attacked the bridge, they forced some civilians in front of them for cover. The civilians broke and fled at the bridge, and Charlie had to go it alone.

The First Military Police Battalion was responsible for the security of the bridge, and Company A was sent down to help. One member of Company A had just got out of the hospital after having malaria. He caught a resupply vehicle to rejoin his Company. "Damn if I'll miss the action!" he said.

The First Sergeant showed me a cigarette lighter he found on one of the enemy dead. "402d Sapper Battalion," he said. "First time we've run into them." The 402d VC Sappers had crossed the river, behind a barrage of mortar and rocket shells, and routed some of the South Vietnamese militia forces. The VC were forced back by the Marines. It was fairly quiet now. By afternoon there was no firing at the bridge, although you could hear some small arms fire in the distance.

I was taking a news correspondent along the Company line to get a story about Recon Marines at the bridge. We missed the turn right at the last position and so continued down the trail with a five-man RVN patrol. We could not speak Vietnamese, and they could not speak English.

"CP," I said, and I pointed down the trail.

"CP," one answered, and nodded in agreement.

After a few hundred meters, I knew there were no other units in the area.

"Better go back," I said to the correspondent.

The RVNs stopped at a small grave site shrine. "VC CP," stated the leader. It was a CP used by Charlie during the attack.

The correspondent took some photos, and we parted company with our Vietnamese allies. It was a lonely walk back, about one thousand meters to our lines. Just the two of us.

"If Charlie opens up now, we've had it," I said.

Returning to the Company lines, we turned left and checked positions. The correspondent found a Marine to interview.

"How do you like this compared to a Recon patrol?"

"I'd rather be Recon."

"Why?"

"Don't like this waiting in one position."

"When did you come off patrol last?"

"Day before yesterday."

"What's the difference?"

"For one, we don't wear helmets or vests on Recon."

"What else?"

"We're on our own, by ourselves."

The correspondent interviewed a few more Marines at their positions as we continued along the line. Finally, we came to the main road in Hoa Vang. A few natives were there trying to clean up the rubble and bury their dead.

It was about five o'clock in the evening when we got the word. "We're going back." The Company First Sergeant began to bark out orders. Recon was being relieved by a Company from the Fifth Marine Regiment.

The street was crowded with vehicles and Marines. Marines moving in and Marines moving out. Vehicles trying to cross the bridge blocked the road. The "grunts" from the Fifth were forming up on the road.

"Tough bunch," said the correspondent, nodding toward the Fifth Marines.

Company A wanted to stay for the finish. The battle for Hoa Vang and Cam Le was about over, and Recon was going back to our area.

"Move out!"

One week later, I was in Hawaii on R&R leave.

"What were you doing at the bridge?" my wife asked.

"I wanted to be sure Charlie didn't get to the air base and mess up my R&R flight," I replied.

11 September 1968*

There's a tangible feeling of special warmth between Sgt.Maj. Jack Jaunal and the kids he meets from home. He usually knows them. In some cases, he recruited them in Burien. He has joined them in Vietnam where they are stationed with the 1st Recon. Bat., 1st Marine Div., on Freedom Hill, near Da Nang.

The motto of 1st Recon, is "Swift, Silent and Deadly." On patrol, they may be all of those things, but in camp, Lance Corporals Rod Hunter, Seattle; Chester Porter, Renton; Bob Gwinn, Auburn, and Corporals John Evans, Kent, and Steve Blackwood, Tacoma – are far from silent.

What do they talk about when they get together with people from home? Jack Jaunal and I know, because all of us sat around his quarters one afternoon.

Like most men – and they are men in spite of their youth, (19 to 22 years old), they talk "shop." They preferred not to be identified, so their conversation follows, just as I recorded it.

"Remember the patrol in Bleach Valley?"

"Hey! Were you on that one?"

"Yeh, it was crazy, man. We'd been in touch with the CP (Command Post), here and they said we had to stay out. They couldn't pick us up because Hill 605 was crawling with VC.

"Cripes, we were right there, making the call from 605 and we didn't see any gooks. (Viet Cong.) We had been out for five days and we wanted to come in."

"Wasn't that when Shorty ripped the seat out of his jungle fatigues (camouflage uniform) and there was almost murder when you got back?" interrupted one who had not been on patrol, but had obviously heard about it.

"Yeah, I just happened to have an instamatic camera. We really harassed him when we got back and I got the roll developed. He could have killed me. It's the most important thing I remember about that operation. My gosh, it was funny."

It wasn't important in the re-telling that they had been without water for three days and without food for two.

"I wish 'Oklahoma Joe,' (another operation), had been that funny," another spoke up. "It was an operation on Hill 257. The third night out the lieutenant put us

*Article entitled "From Where I'm Standing," from *Highline Times*, Burien, Washington, by Ginny Anderson. Reprinted by permission.

on one hundred percent alert. Some rockets came in but they went right over our heads."

"Was this an out post?" I asked.

"Yes, the lieutenant was the CO (Commanding Officer). He was about 23 I guess, then all of a sudden we were hit by about 40 incoming grenades.

"There were two KIAs (Killed in Action) and five wounded. The CO lost an arm and an eye."

"Boy, that was a lot different than 'Hot Pepper.' It turned out to be a cold mother (slang for anything from bombs or the enemy to, as in this case, a patrol). We humped around and all we got was cold and wet. No gooks. No contacts." (Those on a recon patrol are called "humpers" because they "hump" through jungle and rice paddies keeping low).

"One operation, heck, I forget the name of it, but anyway – we were out to make a snatch (take a prisoner). The chopper let us out at the LZ (landing zone), and we headed down this trail and here's this 'co' (Vietnamese for girl).

"She was in Indian (enemy) country, slave labor I guess, 'cause they had stuck her out in front just in case something came up.

"We grabbed her, called the chopper back and put her aboard. We started dee-dee boppin' (running along) down the trail and suddenly – Pow! Pow! There's a bunch of VC.

"We opened up and zapped (hit) 'em with everything we had. We knocked them off except this one little gook who came running down the trail, trying to get away. We grabbed him, too. We'd called for an armed Huey to cover us and they came down. We threw him aboard.

"Our 'bird' (helicopter) came in and extracted us. We just got in and got out. That's a good patrol!"

"I like OP (Out Post, usually on a hill for observation of enemy movements) duty better than humping."

"Who doesn't, except I'd just as soon be someplace else if they are overrun. Hey, Blackwood, didn't you get a Bronze Star on a deal like that?"

Cpl. Steve Blackwood was suddenly mute, although he had been doing a lot of talking. I learned from Sgt.Maj. Jaunal that he had earned the Bronze Star last September, on Operation Swift at Tam Khe.

"They were dug in and the VC were determined to take them," Jaunal said. "They were fighting hard and this one VC ran up and planted their flag."

"Yeh, and we were still there on the hill. We had some wounded and it was pretty hairy (rough, critical) for a little while. But when that little gook figured we were beat and he could plant their flag – that did it. Blackwood mowed him down and the guys following him. As you can see – we got out."

I could see they had gotten out – out of the 'hairiest' situations, some of which would challenge the Hollywood written plots of the most popular TV program in VN – "Combat." (Don't ask me why, but it is.)

But the VC is not their only enemy. Sometimes nature attacks with equal rage. With a sudden thunder and lightning storm the preferred security of the OP vanishes. The same radio equipment that makes them valuable, also attracts deadly lightning. It has killed two and severely burned another in a month of frequent storms.

"No sweat," they say, with a shrug of their shoulders. (No sweat, don't worry about it.)

And so they talk, almost in a foreign language, revealing their youth – and their maturity. They said little of their abilities or accomplishments.

They don't doubt the future. They have plans for going home, getting married or continuing college. Some will extend their tour in Viet Nam or re-enlist. Some will become "lifers" (Career Marines, retiring in 20 years). They express no doubts. They have hunted and met the VC squarely. They know the cunning spread of Communism, the "never had a choice" victims. They express no doubts as to why they are here.

13 September 1968

"What is that ?" I said aloud as I walked over to a bulletin type board with several photographs pinned to it.

"We call it the 'Ugly Board', Sergeant Major."

I was visiting the Battalion Adjutant, Lieutenant Martin, and his Admin Section to see if we were winning the paperwork war.

"Just what is an Ugly Board?" I asked.

The admin clerks explained. The Ugly Board was a group of photographs of several young and not so young women that had written to these and other Marines in the Battalion.

There are many women and girls who want to write to Marines in Vietnam and they list themselves in the *Sea Tiger*, a newspaper published in Nam for Marines.

Several Marines in the Battalion answered, and began writing to the women. Most of the time photographs are exchanged between the writers.

According to an article in the *Sea Tiger*, there is one Marine Sergeant who "corresponds regularly with 77 women." One woman notified the editor that she was writing to 126 Marines, "and she couldn't afford the upkeep of such an extensive pen-pal program." She requested that her name be dropped from the list, not knowing names are only published once. Another woman also wanted to be dropped from the list. She is thirty-one years old and all her Marine writers were younger, eighteen or nineteen. A divorcee, 38, wrote that "her husband went out to see the new models and never returned from the showroom." One woman listed her marital status as "38-26-42." A teenager from Iowa listed thirty-seven qualifications a Marine must possess, and then "enumerates 36 of her own stellar characteristics."

"We're going to see who gets the ugliest picture," states one of the clerks.

"It's a contest," remarks another.

I looked at the photographs with a renewed interest. Some fat ones, a few rather homely. Plain looking women on the most part. Most of them young, maybe too young, and a couple of not so young – like maybe several years older than the Marines they write. I thought to myself, "All looking for husbands."

Most of the photographs were of the outdoor type, several in bathing suits – some rather "busty" types and one poor imitation of a sex symbol.

"How about this one?" I asked, pointing to a fairly attractive looking girl.

"She wrote to Lieutenant -----. It's the best he could do. She really doesn't qualify but he wanted her picture up anyway."

"You wouldn't have a picture for the board, would you, Sergeant Major?" asked one of the clerks.

"No," I replied, "I only have some of Camp Fire Girls and a Drill Team. Every one of them is a good looker. Sorry 'bout that."

Lonely women and lonely Marines – if they only knew. I wonder if there is an "Ugly Marine Board?"

Today I read the *Sea Tiger* "Mail Bag." More than a dozen new candidates' names and addresses appeared.

14 September 1968

The letter I just finished reading was from a worried mother and father in Auburn, Washington. It informed me that they had not heard from their son for over three weeks. He was a Corporal in our Battalion.

Most of the time "no mail" letters are addressed to the Company Commander or First Sergeant. Sometimes they are sent to the Battalion, Regiment, and occasionally – the General.

This one was addressed to me by name. The parents had read my name in a local news release about Recon Battalion. The release mentioned I was the Battalion Sergeant Major, etc.

"Another son," I thought, "who doesn't know the worry he can cause his parents."

I put the letter to one side of my field desk and reached for the field-phone. The Battalion switchboard rang the Company I requested. The Company Clerk answered.

"This is the Battalion Sergeant Major, let me talk to the First Sergeant, please." A few moments pause and, "Yes, Sir, Sergeant Major."

"Say First, do you have a Corporal Gwinn in your Company?"

"Yes, he's in the First Platoon."

"Is he here or in the bush?"

"He's in the area."

"Tell him to report to my office now and on the double."

About five minutes after my telephone call, there was a knock on my screened door. I could see the Corporal standing outside. He was not too sure. It is not very often you are told to report to the Battalion Sergeant Major.

"Come in," I said.

"You wanted to see me, Sergeant Major?"

"Yes," I said as I reached for the letter on my desk. "Stand at ease, Corporal Gwinn."

As I put the letter in front of me, I quietly asked, "When did you write your parents last?"

He didn't remember – a week ago – maybe longer.

I picked up the letter and read from it when his parents received his last letter. I leaned back, looked him hard in the eyes and waited.

He fumbled with a few words and then finished with, "I haven't had time, Sergeant Major. Been on patrol and," he didn't get to finish.

"Don't give me that 'no time' crap," I softly said, and then in a hard tone, "I know how often you go on patrol or OP duty." I continued in a softer tone, "I know how many days you're in the CP area and I also know how many beers are sold at the Enlisted Club. I know you have time for a beer at the 'E' club, don't you?"

"Yes, Sir." He smiled a little.

"You have time for the movie, don't you? And the PX?"

Still looking him hard in the eyes, I leaned forward on my desk and said, "What do you mean you don't have time to write your parents?"

"I see what you mean, Sergeant Major. Guess I just forgot about it."

"I want you to go right back to your quarters and write to your parents, Corporal Gwinn.

"Hell, they don't know what's going on over here. They worry. Can't help it. If the newspapers say anything about Marines in trouble, they wonder if it's you. If they read or

118

hear Marines have been rocketed, they don't know if it's this CP or Saigon. Not knowing is the worst part of a war. And they don't know what is happening over here.

"You know, the hardest part of a war is on the parents, the wives, and families. They have to sweat it out.

"To be honest, we've got it pretty easy, right?"

"I guess you're right, Sergeant Major. Guess I wasn't thinking. No more problems with mail. I'll write regularly from now on."

"Good," I replied.

"Will that be all?"

"Yes, you can shove off."

He turned around and opened the door. As he prepared to step outside I said, "Corporal Gwinn." He turned half around and looked back at me.

"You're not twenty-one yet are you?"

"No," he said, a bit puzzled by the question.

"Marine," I said and pointed a finger in his direction, "next time I get a letter from your parents like this one," pointing to the letter and back at him, "I'm going to write for permission to spank you."

He did not know what to say. His mouth started to open but no words came out, and he had a look of doubt in his eyes. He did not know if I was joking or not.

We stared at each other for a few moments and then he half smiled and I did the same. He continued out the door.

23 September 1968

She was cleaning a Vietnamese civilian woman and it looked like a messy job to me. At first she did not notice me standing off to the side of the bed. She looked up, a look of surprise and then recognition came to her face, followed by a big smile.

"Sergeant Jaunal," she said. It was Lieutenant Commander Lois Nickerson, Navy Nurse Corps. "I'll be with you in a few minutes." We knew each other from our recruiting duty days in Seattle. This was far different duty.

"We should have stayed in Seattle," she said as she left the bedside. As she walked toward me she wiped some stray hairs from in front of her eyes with part of her right arm and I noticed she was wearing rubber surgical gloves.

"How did you know I was here?" she asked.

"Commander Nagy told me. I was visiting some of our wounded on her ward and asked if she knew you."

Because she was on duty and I was on my way back to my outfit, we didn't have much time for a visit. After about ten minutes of questions, answers and reminiscences, I told her it was time for me to shove off. "See you next trip, Commander."

"That's a promise, maybe we can visit longer," she replied.

Commander Nickerson was one of the thirty Navy Nurses assigned to the NSA Hospital, Da Nang. Her duties are basically the same as if she were back in the States.

The major difference in Vietnam is that most of the medical treatment is an emergency and, when the Medevacs arrive, groups of eight to ten wounded at a time require care immediately. Casualties are flown by helicopter to the hospital and are on the operating table in an average of sixty minutes after being wounded. The casualties come to the hospital from all parts of the I Corps Tactical Zone, including the areas along the DMZ.

During the enemy Tet offensive in February, in one single day, 169 patients were treated for wounds and injuries.

It is not uncommon for the nurses to work shifts of twelve or more hours, and if they are lucky, twelve hours off duty.

Commander Mary F. Cannon remarked that the Navy Nurse in Vietnam "can expect to work longer and harder than she ever has in her life, but she will also find her work to be the most satisfying she will ever do."

In this war without front lines, the nurses, Navy or Army, are in the middle of many combat situations. Many times they have had to take to the bunkers during a rocket or mortar attack. Those on ward duty can be found with their patients.

All the Navy Nurses in Vietnam are volunteers. Lieutenant Virginia M. Krall, one of the nurses at Da Nang probably stated it best about the Navy Nurse in Vietnam when she said, "This is what we are paid to do, to nurse the sick and injured back to health, and I can think of no place where we are more needed."

She was right.

10 October 1968

Corporal William D. Nagel (North Haven, Connecticut), of Company A, carries a good luck piece with him that has special meaning. It is a twisted remains of a hand grenade.

Nagel was a member of a reconnaissance patrol in the Happy Valley area south of Da Nang. The patrol was heading toward an objective when they came upon a large open rocky area which had to be crossed.

The patrol began crossing the area. "Our radioman was having some trouble with the rocks," remarked Nagel, "so I stopped to give him some cover."

At the same time the patrol began to take sniper fire from an unknown enemy position. About one hundred rounds flew in their direction. One round pierced a grenade hanging on Nagel's ammo belt, tearing it to shreds. For some unexplainable reason the grenade did not explode.

"It felt like someone hit me in the stomach, but at the time I was more worried about getting out of those rocks and underbrush."

The patrol made it to cover without casualties, but Nagel's call was a little too close. The round missed the grenade's blasting cap by one-eighth of an inch – more or less!

12 October 1968*

Monsoon rains all morning.

13 October 1968*

Some rain, not much. Behind on helicopter lifts.

14 October 1968*

Monsoon rains *all day*. No 'copters flying.

15 October 1968*

Rains most of morning but clear for most of afternoon.

16 October 1968*

Monsoon rains – 6 inches in morning, supposed to last for another 48 hrs. Can't get patrols in or out by air, no 'copters.

*From my Journal. JWJ

17 October 1968*

Da Nang, Vietnam – The battle of Da Nang began as a sneak attack, a thief in the dark. It was a battle for a bridge and a suburb of Da Nang called Cam Le. The telephone wire to the M.P.s on the bridge was cut every night for seven nights before the attack. This was for us a warning.

The Viet-Cong were already swarming in the suburb of Cam Le when the rockets and machine guns of the foe opened up on the bridge at 3 a.m.

Our military police fought back with fury. The bridge tower was hit. A new man in the country ran for a jeep to take cover under it from incoming mortars, but the jeep was hit and went up in flames before he reached it. We held on the north end of the bridge. The enemy took the south end.

When I arrived, Lance Cpl. Harold Walton, Jr., was shooting from the tower of the bridge. During a lull in the fighting, he came down to meet me. He lives in Mountlake Terrace. On his helmet is the name Janice. She lives in Alderwood Manor. His brother, Jack, and his nephew, Frank, are in Vietnam. His brother-in-law, Bill Greene, is coming. His brother, Barrey, just went home.

From a house near the bridge we watched the fighting. Five tanks drew up on the other shore and fired at the enemy-held bunker at the south end of the bridge. A Viet-Cong jumped out and dived into the water.

Marines from all directions ran to the bridge to get a shot at him as he swam downstream away from us. Walton ran, too. The bullets spurted all around the black, bobbing head until it sank.

Then the snipers opened up on us and we ran from the bridge.

Walton told me that eight Marines were pinned down on the other side, one of them Lance Cpl. Walt Henry from the University District of Seattle. Later we learned he got out, wounded.

When the south end of the bridge was secure, we walked across the bridge. The leader on one of the tanks that had knocked out the bunker was Sgt. Roy Groner.

Groner, born in Renton, lives with his mother and sister at 3455 S. 173rd St. He is 24 and has been a marine for 7 ½ years.

---

*Article entitled "Sneak Attack," by Ernie Zaugg, published in *Seattle Times*. Reprinted by permission.

In the village, the people were scurrying into the houses to save their belongings from the flames. A man with a tiny basin was scooping water from a puddle and throwing it toward his blazing home.

A wounded Viet-Cong was lying by the roadside. A Vietnamese policeman stood idly by the groaning enemy. A French correspondent, Jean Marcel Goodstikker, abused the officer in French and English for his lack of humanity. The policeman answered, "OK, OK," and did nothing. Later, Goodstikker told the chief of police about this. He agreed it was bad.

Goodstikker is new to the land. After a time, you get hardened to Asian indifference to suffering. Another Frenchman told me that a Frenchman will charge a policeman at the slightest excuse. This may be the explanation of Goodstikker's zeal.

The men who had been fighting all day came out of the village and sat under the banana trees. They talked of fatigue with concrete, personal expressions as though it were a person or a god. They had three gods: Fear, hunger and fatigue.

So it is with men at war.

The Recon men were setting in for the night in a carpenter's shop. One of them piled the boards for coffins and furniture neatly. The refugees who had fled in the morning were coming back.

Sgt.Maj. Jack Jaunal explained to me that the men were apprehensive because their element was the tree canopy, primeval jungle, where there are only enemy.

"Here they have to distinguish between friend and foe," he said.

Jaunal and his wife live at 1250 S. 159th St., Burien. He is the sergeant major of the First Reconnaissance Battalion. He has had nine months of jungle fighting.

Pfc. James Rickard said, "This city fighting is the most boring thing I have ever done." Rickard's grandparents, Mr. and Mrs. Robert Parson, live in Camas.

The Recon men lost several of their number from heat exhaustion. They are not used to wearing the heavy flak jackets required for city fighting. They did a good job despite being out of their natural element. They were used as a blocking force and let no Viet-Cong through.

Even though evening was falling, the heat was oppressive. The men made some joking remarks about Iceland and how "Siggi" should not have left that nice, cool island. "Siggi" was Pfc. Sigurdur Hjaltason. He was born in Iceland, but now lives at 23006 60th Ave. W., Mountlake Terrace.

In a bunker, a Marine Corps officer said defiantly, "If Charlie hits again tonight, he is one unhappy S.O.B."

"Or crazy," said another marine.

"When he kills four Marines, he thinks that is a big thing."

"He killed more than that."

"Maybe seven. When he kills 10, he is a noisy, little man."

It is a strange war. You watch fighting all day, then return to the center of town, where you feel safe, though you hear a lot of shooting and the buildings shake from the big guns. Then you have a beer and for a moment forget the war.

18 October 1968*

Back to rains, almost all day, not as heavy. Couple teams three days overdue.

1300 – Gen Lemay for briefing on Recon – plenty of security.

19 October 1968*

Got two patrols in, 3 days overdue because of bad weather. Tired, wet & hungry.

20 October 1968*

Memorial Services 1800 hours for Marine killed by fire, burns. Marine was OK when Colonel and I visited him at hospital, was in spirits. By the time we got back to CP, was info'd Marine had died.

31 October 1968*

Went with scuba divers on bridge checks, 5 bridges.

*From my Journal. JWJ

2 November 1968

One of our Recon patrols led by Sergeant S.N. Farris recently added insult to injury when Marines left a sign bearing a big black ace of spades and the message "Recon Was Here" at an NVA bunker complex they had destroyed.

The Patrol was on a mission deep in NVA territory southwest of Da Nang when they spotted signs of the enemy in the area. "We came upon a well used trail and the brush nearby was matted down," said Farris.

The Marines followed the trail up an embankment and came upon a cluster of seven well constructed huts which proved to be an NVA platoon-sized base camp.

"We didn't see any people at first," remarked a patrol member, Private First Class D.M. Hodge, "but there were plenty of livestock and domestic animals around."

Under the huts was a tunnel complex leading to a bunker approximately six feet square. An old woman was found in one of the tunnels. The Marines persuaded her to leave, and as they were leading her from the tunnel, the patrol came under enemy fire from a nearby treeline. The Marines returned fire and the enemy fled.

A search of the base camp yielded approximately five hundred pounds of food and a large supply of tobacco. The Marines also discovered khaki uniforms, a supply of medical equipment, a large quantity of insulin, and four enemy weapons.

The Recon Marines destroyed the bunker, and then moved about 400 meters away and set up an ambush site. They surprised a group of eight enemy soldiers and opened fire. When the firefight was over, the Marines searched the area and found several blood trails, two packs containing mortar rounds and grenades, and several documents.

The next morning, the patrol scouted the enemy camp again. The Marines found that their sign had been turned around and several Vietnamese words had been scrawled on it. However, the Marines could not read the message. "But," remarked Private First Class T.J. Sales, "it sure looked nasty."

7 November 1968*

Had first KIA since August – Sgt from Force, almost blown in half by grenade. Went to ID body at Med Battalion.

The Sergeant had been the Battalion police NCO and wanted to "be in the bush" with our Recon patrols. "Why?" I asked him, even though I knew the answer. I supported his request for reconnaissance duty – hell – I remembered how I felt during WWII. He came to see me before his first patrol. "Got my transfer, Sergeant Major. Thanks for your help." Now he was dead – from his chest to his groin was a big hole.

10 November 1968*

Marine Corps birthday, 193 years old – ceremony – visited hospital patients and brig.

12 November 1968*

Bad accident – grenade went off on LZ, killed two Marines, two in serious condition, five wounded, two with small cuts, wounds. Visited wounded in hospital.

*From my Journal. JWJ

❀

14 November 1968

It was a hot afternoon and I was standing at the ships' landing in Da Nang harbor waiting for the launch that would take me out to the hospital ship. I was going to visit one of the wounded Marines from our Battalion.

On the road nearby, a jeep pulled off to the side and a figure stepped out. Small swirls of dust settled around the wheels of the jeep and the departing passenger's boots. He stepped to the side of the road and gave a gesture of "Thanks for the ride."

He turned from the jeep and started walking toward the dock. He was wearing the standard jungle uniform being worn in Vietnam, and was dusty from the helmet on his head to the toes of his parachute boots. On the left shoulder of his uniform was the combat patch of the First Air Cavalry Division, and above his left pocket, the wings of a senior parachutist. Three chevrons up and the three rockers below with a diamond in the center indicated his rank of First Sergeant.

His walk seemed a little weary as if he was carrying a pack or great weight that caused his shoulders to sag forward a little. I estimated he had twenty plus years service – another old soldier in another war.

As he neared me I spoke, "How goes it, First?"

He looked at me and then took a step closer. "OK," he noticed my rank, "Sergeant Major." He had a leathery face from years of soldiering and grey hair in his eyebrows. "Going to the ship?" he asked.

131

"Yes," I replied, "I've got a wounded Marine out there."

"Me too. My son."

"Bad?"

"Don't know really." He removed his helmet and wiped some dirt from his face. His hair was iron grey. He put his helmet back on and reached inside one of his pockets. "Smoke?"

"No thanks," I replied. We didn't speak for a few minutes. After a few puffs on his cigarette he said, "My son's a Marine."

"How did that grab you?" I asked.

"Didn't like it at all. Wanted him to go to West Point. I've been Army enlisted for twenty-five years. Wanted him to be an officer but it didn't work out."

We watched a South Vietnamese soldier and his girl ride by on a Honda.

"What happened?" I asked.

"Decided he wanted to join the Marines. Tougher outfit, he figured. It was lucky the wife and I got him to finish high school. Guess he wanted to get some medals and show up the old man." There was a pause and then, "He's got himself a medal now."

The launch arrived from the hospital ship. The old soldier tore apart what was left of his cigarette and let the ashes and tobacco drop to the ground.

"Young troopers don't know how to field strip anymore."

The young Marine was lying on a lower bunk with that one-thousand-inch stare the wounded sometimes have. His eyes came into focus as he looked up and noticed the old soldier standing by his bunk. The word was almost like a question, "Dad."

"Hi, son."

They didn't say anything for a few seconds. The ward nurse, a small redhead, watched for a moment and then continued talking to one of the corpsmen. I was a short distance away talking to the wounded Marine from our

Battalion. At times I could hear some of the nearby conversation.

"I thought Marines were tough?"

"Guess I'm not as tough as I thought."

"How did it happen?"

"Rockets. Hit us one night and I couldn't outrun the piece that got me."

"How's Mom?"

"Worried. Don't know if she is worried more about you or me."

"Guess I'll beat you home so that leaves only you."

"Might as well go myself. Only stayed to help you jarheads out."

It was later when the redheaded nurse came around to tell us when the launch would be going back. Seemed like a short visit. Guess we talked longer than we thought.

The old soldier prepared to leave. The father and son looked at each other and tried to sound casual as they spoke. Underneath they were probably all choked up; there seemed to be a slight tremble in their voices. There were no goodbyes, only a "So long, See ya, take care," and a handshake.

The old soldier turned around and walked out of the ward without looking back. I had just finished talking to a corpsman as he passed. With a casual "Thank you" salute to the redheaded nurse, I followed the old soldier down the passageway.

He never said a word on our way back to the dock and I asked no questions. We each had our own thoughts.

As we walked from the dock toward the road I asked if he needed a lift. My vehicle was parked several feet away. "No thanks. I should have a ride coming here soon." When he looked at me, tears were beginning to form in his eyes. He said, "I pray God takes care of him."

I felt a little misty eyed myself.

"Take care of yourself, Top Soldier," and I put out my hand. He took it and then clasped his left hand on top. For a few seconds we were just two fathers clasping hands.

"See ya, Sergeant Major – and thanks."

As I drove off I could see him smoking a cigarette and looking in the direction of the hospital ship.

16 November 1968*

Took CBS News camera crew on bridge checks.

17 November 1968*

Rockets in Da Nang area – hit Da Nang Airbase, also Shore Party Battalion 1.5 miles from us – other areas hit.
Team in contact, two WIAs.
Visited WIAs at First Med Battalion.

18 November 1968*

Visited NSA Hospital.
Two patrols in contact today.

20 November 1968*

Visited Hospital; man had finger blown off by accident while on ambush patrol.
Forming provisional infantry battalion again in case needed –
Charlie out stirring up trouble.

*From my Journal. JWJ

21 November 1968

It was almost zero seven-thirty; the companies would be forming up for the morning formation. I was having my second cup of coffee at the Staff NCO mess. It was empty except for the messmen, a First Sergeant, a Gunny, and me. As I was drinking my coffee, I was looking out the windows overlooking the fields and Battalion area. My eyes caught something in the air. Around the object the air looked "warped," like heat waves from a toaster. By the time my eyes relayed what I saw to my brain, I thought "rockets" – BOOM! It hit near the mess. Smoke and dirt raised in the air as my coffee cup came down.

"Take it easy!" I yelled as cooks and messmen ran for the door. You could hear the rockets – BOOM! The First Sergeant and Gunny departed. I decided to stay put and laid on the deck – a buzz overhead and BOOM!

"I hope my luck holds out."

A short pause and more overhead. I went outside to check for any injured. I could see the smoke, two together and one farther out. Our Battalion area is on the side of a hill. I looked down toward Company A. The First Sergeant was checking his bunkers.

"Sergeant Major, we had better get nipping!" he yelled.

"I say First, did you see the dirty devils that done this dastardly deed?" I replied.

Everything OK at Company A. A few more faces came out from the embankment below me.

"Guess it is over?" said one.

136

"I hope," replied the other.

I double-timed toward Company C. "Anyone hurt?"

A few Marines were looking at the spot a rocket hit.

"One landed in Motor Tee," said a Marine. The motor transport park is above the mess hall. The rocket destroyed two jeeps and trailers.

"Thirty meters lower and it would have been in our coffee!" I thought to myself.

Rocket fragments had landed throughout the area. One piece landed in the "In" basket of the Company C office. A wheel from one of the jeeps landed down hill about 200 meters into Company E's area. The First Sergeant from Echo went up to see the Motor Transport Sergeant and told him not to toss "his trash in my Company area."

Two rockets landed at the bottom of the hill, just off the LZ. The concussion blew out the plastic window in the chapel. A large piece of shrapnel went through the roof of a hut in Company D and landed on one Marine's rack. He has it for a souvenir now. The First Sergeant of Company B counted nine rounds. One small fragment went across the arm of Private First Class W.R. Hutchens (Auburn, Washington), a Headquarters Company clerk.

The rocket attack was over and the sea stories began. We could see smoke from the Eleventh Marines area (an artillery unit). One rocket landed on a helicopter, killing two men.

Our Battalion Communications Sergeant walked by, mud from head to toe. He found a wet ditch to jump into.

Our casualties were light – small slivers of shrapnel in a few Marines and one corpsman. One Marine from Company C had a small piece in his thigh and had to spend a week in the hospital.

One of our patrols came in. "Maybe we had better go back out. It may be safer!"

29 November 1968*

Men of the 1st Reconnaissance Bn., SCUBA team have set a III Marine Amphibious Force record during the past three months.

The four-man team had made 280 underwater security checks of bridges essential to the main supply routes within the 1st Marine Division's Tactical Area of Responsibility (TAOR).

The team consists of SSgt. C.E. Hatton (607 Pasco Ave., Dade City, Fla.), team leader. His assistants are Cpl. D.C. Baker (27 Center Lane, Centerville, Mass.), Cpl. J.T. Egan (6933 Chevy Chase Way, Sacramento, Calif.), and Cpl. A.L. Morris (Versailles, Mo.).

They are constantly on the alert for underwater enemy explosive devices, floating mines, a backlog of debris against pilings and other signs of bridge insecurity such as broken or cracked piling.

The Recon Leathernecks travel throughout the Division area with air tanks, wet suits, flippers, masks and other tools of their trade stopping just long enough at each bridge to don their diving gear and search out the murky waters.

In addition to their "routine" bridge checks, members of the team have taken part in many long range clandestine patrols deep into enemy territory.

They often accompany infantry units on patrols near rivers with the responsibility of checking for hidden weapons caches and underwater cave entrances.

During the past two months these underwater teams have recovered three bodies, two tons of ordnance and numerous weapons, both Allied and enemy, including a 140mm enemy rocket.

In preparing for their strenuous tasks, the SCUBA** Marines attend a three-week Navy Scuba school in either Florida or the Philippines. Here in Vietnam, they conduct an extensive physical conditioning program to keep in shape. The divers often pit their strength against each other to build up their swimming muscles which require the greatest amount of individual discipline and stamina while swimming.

*News article from *Sea Tiger* by Gunnery Sergeant C. Lane
**See Glossary

30 November 1968*

The pilot of the Huey gunship came over to the Colonel (Lieutenant Colonel L.P. Charon, New York) and asked if he still wanted to go in "if we take enemy fire?"

"It's up to you, you're the pilot."

"If it is just sniper fire we'll still go in," replied the pilot, "otherwise we won't."

Today was the tenth day of Operation Meade River, which was to continue until 9 December. It was the largest assault helicopter lift in the history of the Corps – and one large success in a lost war.*

The Colonel, the First Sergeant from Company B, one of his corpsmen, and I climbed aboard the aircraft. We were on our way to recover the bodies of three Recon Marines. They had been scouting out a bunker complex when the enemy opened up on them.

The rest of the patrol managed to get some air support and a helicopter came in for the wounded. The Medevac 'copter came in and one of the crewmen was shot through the leg. They got the wounded Marine but another Medevac 'copter was hit in the oil line and went down in the paddy. A Reaction Force was sent in to guard the downed bird. In the meantime a Huey came in and picked up our wounded corpsman (Hospitalman Third Class Henry Grant USN, Columbus, Montana). The remainder of the Recon patrol stayed with the Reaction Force overnight.

* See article from *Marine Corps GAZETTE*, pp. 153-154, *Vietnam '68: Jack's Journal*. Reprinted by permission.

As the gunship started down, I noticed the rain drops on the windshield; the ground started to turn around as we came in low – touchdown. The Colonel and I jumped from one side and the First Sergeant and corpsman from the other. We started our run through the paddy as the bird took off.

In places the water was up to our knees as we ran toward the Marines guarding the downed bird. We found two of the Recon Marines and asked for the patrol leader.

"He went out to get the bodies," one of them replied.

The patrol leader was showing the CO of Company I, Twenty-sixth Marines, where the bodies should be near the bunker complex. It was about 200 plus meters out, in the tree line. Most of the company were out recovering the bodies. The rest were guarding the downed bird, while the air crew worked on it. The ground was wet, water ankle deep in most places and elephant grass about four feet high around the paddy. We could not do anything except wait, talk, and listen to small arms fire. We could also see an air strike in progress.

"Here they come."

The Company had just left the tree line – three groups of Marines in the center rear, carrying those green ponchos with the bodies inside. The Colonel introduced himself to the Company officers.

"I'm Lieutenant Colonel Charon."

"Sorry we couldn't get them sooner Colonel." It was the Company Commander speaking. "We didn't find their rifles, Charlie took them. He left their bodies alone."

I noticed the patrol leader, a Sergeant; he had tears in his eyes. It was tough on him.

We sat down to wait for a helicopter. The First Sergeant, R.J. Maughan, was talking to his Marines. The corpsman was operating the radio.

"You're getting too short for this, Doc," I said. The doc just smiled; he told me before we took off they were "his men." He and the First Sergeant managed to find the Colonel and me just before takeoff. "Got room for us?" That's when I first asked him if he wasn't too short for this – he was due to go home soon. Doc is Hospitalman Second Class Lloyd Ellis, USN, Las Vegas, New Mexico.

The sun came out and it got a little warm; a cool breeze blew the elephant grass to one side. A Marine had his boot off, drying a foot, one at a time. If anything happened fast, he would be half ready to go.

"Trying to beat immersion foot."

We waited.

A tired rifleman had found a small mound of earth out of the water and crawled into a small human ball and tried to sleep.

"Pilots must be at chow."

After a short time we saw them. Four birds and gunships.

"They're going to pick up the 'copter first." It was the Company radio operator passing the word.

"Helmets and jackets on," shouted the Company Gunny.

The Marines got their gear on and faced outboard in case Charlie fired on the birds. The perimeter was around the downed bird. A large H-46 came in for the disassembled parts and crew.

"Any word of our bird?" asked the Colonel.

"None yet."

"Get on the radio and call back."

The infantry was going to move back about 250 meters. That meant the bodies would have to be carried.

A big bird, H-53, came in and lifted out the downed helicopter. More than one camera popped out among the Marines.

"Get ready, one's going to take you out!"

We headed for the bird. The bodies were placed in the aisle, we signaled "thumbs up," the tail closed and we took off.

I looked around. One of the patrol had that thousand-inch stare. Somehow he was not hit. He had been with the three lying on the deck. It was four hours before he got away.

Air through the open parts helped blow away the smell of death, but not quite. The wind started to blow the ponchos and uncover the bodies so we had to hold them down with our hands or feet. I noticed the farthest one back looked asleep on his side with an arm beside his cheek. A small trickle of blood moved along the deck from the second one. It mixed with dirt and turned from red to a rust color. The one in front of me was on his side, knees up, and I had to hold the poncho around him and let him lie against one leg for support. It made the flight back to our LZ uncomfortable, but that was about all I could do for him now.

5 December 1968

The upper half of the walls of my hut are screened like many buildings in the tropical climate. It helps keep the inside cool and provides me a good view of the Battalion area. During the monsoons I can drop side "flaps" down to keep out the rain.

I was sitting at my field desk trying to write an awards recommendation when I noticed movement out of the corner of my left eye. A Civil War soldier passed the screened side of my office! I got up from behind my field desk and looked out the door. It was one of our Recon Marines getting ready for patrol duty. Atop his head was an olive drab replica of a Civil War cap, stovepipe top and small visor in front, tailor made.

"Damn," I thought, "when are we going to get jungle utilities?"

At the time, none of our Recon Marines had been issued the new jungle uniforms and many of them had bought the tiger striped camouflage uniforms of the RVN forces. Others wore the regulation Marine green utility uniform when on patrol.

In the Battalion area, only the regulation cap was authorized. But when on patrol in the bush, Recon Marines could wear almost anything on their heads. Most of the Recon Marines liked the RVN jungle hat or berets. Several wore their Marine issued field cap – some starched!

Other types of headgear included:

The Pirate, a green or camouflage cloth tied around the top of their head.

Duck Hunter, a small brimmed field hat, front down and back up. Privates First Class W. Evans Jr. (Montclair, New Jersey) and D. Crowe (Tucson, Arizona), both of Company D, favored this hat.

Collegiate, a small brimmed field hat turned up all around.

Fore and Aft, the brim of the jungle hat was turned up in front and back, as favored by Gunnery Sergeant T.F. Sparks (Etowah, Tennessee), the First Sergeant of Company D. This was especially popular with the new jungle hat.

Aussie, a large brimmed Australian-type bush hat with the side turned up. Sometimes the side was pinned up with a black Marine Corps emblem.

Safari, a large brimmed Australian-type bush hat with the brim turned down all around. This type was favored by Corporal W.D. Paul (Paul Valley, Oklahoma). His buddy, Lance Corporal J.S. Grandusky (Olean, New York) favored the "duck hunter." Both Marines are members of Company B and just returned from the bush.

The Cowboy, the new jungle hat with the sides turned up and creased on the crown. A favorite.

The Beret, favored by Private First Class W.G. Burton (Peoria, Illinois) of Company A.

Sombrero, the new jungle hat with the brim turned up all around.

Old Corps, the new jungle hat shaped like the Marine Corps campaign hat of yesteryear. My favorite.

After the new jungle uniform was issued, the various individual headgear for the bush faded away.

*20 December 1968**

DA NANG, Vietnam – Generally used in a derogatory manner, the adage "turn about is fair play" proved highly advantageous for a Marine Corps sergeant major in Vietnam.

A year ago, SgtMaj. Jack W. Jaunal served as acting chairman of "Christmas Vietnam '67" – sponsored by the Seattle-King County chapter of the American Red Cross. The program was set up to accumulate gifts from King County residents and send them to Vietnam for Christmas. Because of Jaunal's duties as a recruiter in Seattle, he was asked to help organize the program.

With Jaunal's help, the organization sent more than 6,000 gifts to American forces last Christmas.

This year, he is on the receiving end of "Christmas Vietnam '68." Because of his aid last year, Jaunal has received more than 1,000 gifts for his battalion, the 1st Recon, this Christmas.

---

* From *Fleet Home Town News* (Fleet Home Town News Center, NS, Great Lakes, Illinois). Item in public domain.

24 December 1968

'Twas the night before Christmas and all through
my bunker, my buddies were snoozing, a less-than-
sound slumber.
   Our stockings were hung to dry from the ceiling
and mosquitoes were biting the bites that were healing.
   And I in fatigues and a pot on my head, was
thinking of home and a warm, cozy bed.
   When out to my flank, in a cut field of fire, I
spotted some movement, first low and then higher.
   I started to stare, then remembered by training
"Night vision is better when eyes are not straining."
   As the object approached I was glad that the sound
was not like the scream of an incoming round.
   I gasped with surprise as the object grew nearer,
the image of Santa grew clearer and clearer.
   Traditional suit and a beard flowing white
I shook Joe beside me to witness the sight.
   A man and his reindeer, a sleigh full of cheer, just
as we remembered from Christmas last year.
   But spirits declined as he passed overhead.
We'd hoped he would land, but he di di'd instead.

-Anonymous

25 December 1968

I was calling from the field telephone at the LZ.

"Where's the chow?"

"It's being loaded on the truck now, Sergeant Major."

"Hurry it up, we're behind schedule now!"

I hung up the telephone and walked back to the 'copters. One of the pilots had a piece of white chalk and was printing "MERRY CHRISTMAS" on one side of his bird.

"The troops will probably enjoy that."

Underneath the window on the pilot's side was printed, "Santa Claus Special." And in front, on the nose, was a large printed "HO-HO."

It was Christmas 1968 in Vietnam. The Battalion Chaplain (Lieutenant J.K. Godie, USNR, Renton, Washington), a cook, a couple of other Marines, and I were making a Christmas flight to all of our OPs with hot chow – turkey and all. I also had ten cartoons of goodies from the Knights of Columbus and O-Ki-Hi Camp Fire Girls in Seattle. After a week of field rations, the goodies and hot chow would be welcome.

The chow truck arrived from the mess hall and we loaded up. The chopper warmed up, the tail gate closed and we took off.

First stop was Hill 200; a platoon from Company B was on it. The hill is about eighteen miles south of Da Nang. Last time Charlie tried to take it was on the twenty-first of August. The battle lasted nine and one-half hours. We still own it. As we flew over we could see the yellow smoke marker. We

circled in. It was a nice warm, sunny day, and most of the
Marines were bare chested. We landed and unloaded fast
while the guards manned their positions. Charlie likes to fire
on the birds, and the pilots don't like to sit too long. We
unloaded the birds and they took off, to circle overhead while
we passed out chow, mail and assorted goodies. We had five
minutes on the ground to wish a Merry Christmas and hear
a few words from the Chaplain. Then the birds came back
for us.

On top of the bunker was a Christmas tree – of sorts. The
decorations consisted of belted machine gun ammo, a boot,
cans, and any object you could find on outpost duty.

"Damn, real cookies!"

"Remember, Camp Fire Girls grow to be big girls."

"Birds coming in."

"Time to shove off."

"Merry Christmas."

"Thanks."

The birds landed and we ran aboard. Thumbs up, and we
headed for Hill 146 and the Marines from Company E. Hill
146 is about the same as Hill 200 except the area to land on
is smaller. The landing area is in the middle of the OP and
not very much room for a helicopter. As the birds circled
overhead we passed out gifts and made like Santa's helpers.
We gave the Marines a small Christmas tree sent to me by a
retired Marine Colonel's wife. It was the only Christmas tree
on Hill 146. As we flew off we could see some of the Marines
starting to eat.

Hill 425 was next; that would be Company D. It wasn't
much larger than the last one but at least the landing zone
was down from the bunkers. Again we passed out the
packages. As a young Sergeant broke open some cookies he
asked, "Just how many Camp Fire Girls do you know anyway,
Sergeant Major?"

"Hundreds," I replied, "and they all have big sisters."

A big smile lit up his face and he said, "Sergeant Major, I'm going home with you."

A few more words, the Chaplain spoke, we climbed aboard our birds and took off for Ba Na, one mile in the air. It was cool going up there.

"Clouds all around."

"Wonder if it will be socked in?"

At times Ba Na is socked in and we cannot get aircraft in for days. One time we had a platoon up there for twenty-one days before the weather cleared enough to fly in.

Today the clouds were closing in.

"Looks as if we can make it."

An open spot and the bird started in – we could see Marines begin to gather at the landing zone. As we unloaded, I got word from the pilot – low on gas; can't return for another takeoff. "Besides the clouds are moving in."

The Chaplain cut his greeting short and we boarded the aircraft. I did not have time to see the tree I gave Private First Class William G. Burton (Peoria, Illinois), to put up when his platoon from Company A came up. It was one of several small trees sent to the Battalion for the Christmas holiday. We flew back to the lowlands to refuel at Hill 55.

"One more stop. Dong Den, if we can get in."

The paddies were green; it was a nice sunny day, sort of peaceful from the air. As we climbed over the ridges it got cooler, almost cold. We were under clouds and then above them. I looked out the side and could see the jungle below, clouds all around.

"I hope the pilot can see better than I can. I can't see anything."

Dong Den was manned by Company C Marines and looked like we might not get in. No sunshine there; too many clouds. An opening – we went in – nice try – we touched down and were off again. We tried again. Marines below guided us in – over – a little more – more – down – hold it – OK –

149

touchdown. We were on the ground. I realized how small a spot the LZ is. "Damn good pilot."

This would be a fast stop. Unload, a few words and we were off before the clouds closed in. We swooped down, fast, under the clouds and then – sunshine.

"Made them all," I shouted.

The pilot looked back and gave me a big grin and a "thumbs up." Before we left our LZ, he said we would make them all and we did.

Back to the area and a Christmas meal except for the patrols in the bush. I am finished playing Santa Claus this year. But it did make a Christmas worthwhile.

So it was – Christmas in Vietnam 1968.

Epilogue

It has been twenty years since these stories were first written. Some are as fresh in my mind as the day they happened while others are less remembered. Each is a reminder, a reminiscence, of Vietnam 1968.

Sometimes I still see the body of the young Marine Sergeant who was almost blown in half by an enemy grenade. And Staff Sergeant Hughes telling me, "They're going to get us killed, Sergeant Major." Many names and faces have been forgotten over the years.

Some of the notes, letters, and names I saved have been lost in my travels and only a short sentence, or a few words are recorded in my Journal.

I lost the address of the young wife in Pittsburgh and have been unable to tell her about the 8mm movie film I have that shows her husband a few days before he was killed.

Sergeant Rabenort, Squad Leader of the Reaction Squad for "Heat & Steam," was awarded the Bronze Star Medal.

Sergeant Tidwell returned to his wife in Houston and managed to visit me, along with Lance Corporal Christensen, at Recon before he left.

Lieutenant Colonel B.C. Stinemetz retired as a Colonel and now lives in Washington State.

Lieutenant Colonel L.P. Charon retired a few years after he returned from Vietnam.

Lieutenant Martin is retired and lives in Norfolk, Virginia.

First Sergeant Otis Barker retired after thirty years in the Corps and lives on Okinawa.

Lois Nickerson was a Captain of Navy Nurses and stationed at the Naval Hospital, Annapolis, Maryland, the last I heard.

Gunnery Sergeant Lane, who wrote about Recon's scuba team, retired as a Master Sergeant and went to live in Grants Pass, Oregon.

Former Corporal Gwinn is now married and lives in Renton, Washington. I visited his parents a few years ago and talked to him on the telephone.

Hospitalman Third Class Henry Grant, USN, was recovering from his wounds at the Navy Hospital, Bremerton, Washington, when I visited him last. His wife was living outside the gate and visiting him every day. They planned to return to Montana to live.

Lieutenant Colonel Robert E. Haebel was a Brigadier General and the Commanding General of Force Troops, Fleet Marine Force, Atlantic, Camp Lejeune, North Carolina, when I visited him last. He is now a retired Major General of Marines.

In a *Seattle Times* special travel report by Terry McDermott (July 13, 1986), he wrote, "We climb inside Marble Mountain, to caverns that served as a Viet Cong hospital even while Americans staked out artillery positions above."

After three wars, twelve campaigns, and over thirty-three years military service, I was retired from the Marine Corps on 1 May 1978. At the time, I was Sergeant Major of the Fleet Marine Force, Atlantic, Norfolk, Virginia. The formal ceremony for my relief and retirement was held on 26 April 1978 – ten years from the date I noticed a small piece of blood-stained cloth being taken from the dead body of a young Recon Marine.

One large success in a lost war*

By SgtMaj Jack W. Jaunal, USMC (Ret.)

Operation MEADE RIVER began 10 years ago this month, on 20 November 1968. The Corps had celebrated its 193rd birthday ten days earlier, and this would be the first major operation for the 194th year.

It began with the largest assault helicopter lift in the history of the Corps. When it ended on 9 December 1968, over 1,000 of the enemy had been killed.

The area of operation, which surrounded the village of Dien Ban, in Quang Nam Province, had long been a stronghold for hardcore Vietcong and elements of the 36th North Vietnam Army Regiment. It was considered a continuous approach route to Da Nang through which came the majority of attacks – rocket, mortar and on the ground.

As a combined operation in support of the Government of Vietnam's accelerated pacification campaign, the primary mission was to root out the enemy infrastructure and destroy the enemy, both NVA and VC, and his fortifications. A cordon was to be emplaced around the area, about eleven square miles from which the civilian populace was evacuated for screening by RVN forces and agencies.

The mission was assigned to the 1st Marine Regiment, reinforced by supporting arms and other units: seven battalions of Marines; 1st Battalion, 1st Marines, 2d and 3d Battalions of the 5th Marines, 1st and 2d Battalions of the 7th Marines, and 2d and 3d Battalions of the 26th Marines, plus two battalions of the Army of the Republic of Vietnam's 51st Regiment and two companies of the 2d Korean Marine Brigade.

The helicopter force consisted of more than 75 helicopters, CH-46 Sea Knight and CH-53** Sea Stallion transports, escorted by Huey gunships. They landed Marines at 47 landing zones in a three by eight-mile area while overhead, jet attack and OV-10A Bronco observation aircraft flew on station.

There was no preliminary bombardment by aircraft or artillery to alert the enemy. Marines landed and rushed into defensive positions and prepared for battle. The cordon was tight. The enemy was surrounded.

The Marines and their allies moved thoroughly and effectively. There was no need to hurry. None of the enemy had been able to get out. They tried. Surrounded with no chance to escape they fought tenaciously. The terrain was wet and soggy, rice paddies and tree lines. The Marines searched and probed everything and everywhere. Republic of Vietnam forces moved into the area. Loudspeakers announced the operations and one-half million pamphlets were dropped overhead by low flying aircraft. The villagers were told what to do. They would have three days

*Reprinted from the November 1978 issue of the *Marine Corps GAZETTE.*

**See Glossary

to move to a central collection point. They would bring enough food for one day. One member of each family would be allowed to remain in their house to prevent looting. Livestock would remain behind.

The government of Vietnam would provide food after the first day and the transportation to the central collection point.

Each Vietnamese resident of the area presented identification papers. They were checked, screened and questioned. Individual photographs were taken and new identification cards issued. During the procedure, those who could not provide positive identification were detained for further questioning. Over 2,530 Vietnamese civilians were fed, entertained, cared for and then returned to their searched-and-cleared villages.

As the operation came to a close, two pockets of enemy resistance remained. One, an estimated 40-man force, was well-emplaced in a bunker complex partially concealed and protected by a tree line. The second pocket was a series of huge bunker complexes. The remnants of the 36th NVA Regiment were dug in and prepared to fight to the death. A captured NVA soldier stated that his comrades were well-armed and had plenty of ammunition.

Naval gunfire and Marine artillery hammered at the enemy positions. Marines jets strafed and bombed. An Army psychological operations team, accompanied by Vietnamese interpreters, urged the NVA to surrender. They refused.

The Marine and his rifle, fighting from bunker to bunker, and hole to hole, defeated the last of the enemy. Operation MEADE RIVER was over.

By virtue of the authority vested in me as President of the United States and as Commander-in-Chief of the Armed Forces of the United States, I have today awarded

THE PRESIDENTIAL UNIT CITATION (NAVY)

FOR EXTRAORDINARY HEROISM TO

FIRST MARINE REGIMENT (REINFORCED),
FIRST MARINE DIVISION (REINFORCED),
FLEET MARINE FORCE

For exceptionally meritorious and heroic achievement during the period 20 November to 9 December 1968 in connection with operations against enemy forces in Quang Nam Province, Republic of Vietnam. Participating in Operation MEADE RIVER, a combined operation in support of the Government of Vietnam's Accelerated Pacification Campaign, the First Marine Regiment (Reinforced) skillfully utilized foot and motor transportation, along with the largest assault helicopter lift in Marine Corps history, to successfully emplace a cordon around an eleven-square-mile area from which the civilian populace was evacuated for screening by province and district agencies. Following the establishment of the virtually impenetrable cordon, the Marines commenced to fan out from their positions along the eastern edge of the encirclement to conduct a systematic sweep and search operation in order to ferret out the entrapped enemy. For the next several days, the First Marine Regiment (Reinforced) relentlessly pressed the attack in a series of intense and fierce engagements against an extremely stubborn foe, resulting in a resounding victory for the friendly forces and extensive enemy losses in personnel, supplies and equipment. By their superb professionalism, valiant fighting spirit, and unflagging devotion to duty throughout Operation MEADE RIVER, the officers and men of the First Marine Regiment (Reinforced) made a significant contribution to United States efforts in Southeast Asia and upheld the highest traditions of the Marine Corps and of the United States Naval Service.

Richard Nixon

By virtue of the authority vested in me as President of the United States and as Commander-in-Chief of the Armed Forces of the United States, I have today awarded

THE PRESIDENTIAL UNIT CITATION (NAVY)

FOR EXTRAORDINARY HEROISM TO

FIRST MARINE DIVISION (REINFORCED), FLEET MARINE FORCE

For extraordinary heroism and outstanding performance of duty in action against enemy forces in the Republic of Vietnam from 16 September 1967 to 31 October 1968. Operating primarily in Quang Nam Province, the First Marine Division (Reinforced) superbly executed its threefold mission of searching for and destroying the enemy, defending key airfields and lines of communication, and conducting a pacification and revolutionary development program unparalleled in the annals of warfare. With the Division responsible for over 1,000 square miles of territory, it extended protection and pacification to more than one million Vietnamese. The countless examples of courage, resourcefulness, and dedication demonstrated by the officers and men of the First Marine Division attest to their professionalism and esprit de corps. Their combat activities were skillfully carried out in the face of adverse weather and difficult terrain such as canopied jungles, rugged mountains, swampy lowlands, and hot, sandy beaches. During the enemy Tet-offensive in late January of 1968, the First Marine Division dealt a devastating blow to enemy forces attempting to attack Danang. Again, in May 1968, the Division totally crushed an enemy drive directed against the Danang area through the Go Noi Island region southwest of Danang. The Division achieved this resounding victory through the skillful coordination of ground forces, supporting arms, and aircraft support. Most action in the I Corps Tactical Zone during August of 1968 was centered in the First Marine Division's tactical area of responsibility. The enemy, now looking for a victory which would achieve some measure of psychological or propaganda value, again mounted an attack of major proportions against Danang but were thoroughly repulsed, sustaining heavy casualties. The valiant fighting spirit, perseverance, and teamwork displayed by First Marine Division personnel throughout this period reflected great credit upon themselves and the Marine Corps, and were in keeping with the highest traditions of the United States Naval Service.

THE SECRETARY OF THE NAVY
WASHINGTON

   The Secretary of the Navy takes pleasure in presenting the NAVY UNIT COMMENDATION to

FIRST RECONNAISSANCE BATTALION (REINFORCED)
FIRST MARINE DIVISION (REINFORCED)

for service as set forth in the following

CITATION:

   For exceptionally meritorious service against the insurgent communist (Viet Cong) forces in the Republic of Vietnam from 1 October 1967 to 1 October 1968. During this period, the First Reconnaissance Battalion (Reinforced) supported 22 infantry battalion-size or larger operations and conducted 1,333 patrol missions deep within Viet Cong controlled territory gathering invaluable information regarding Viet Cong activities, techniques, routes of communication, harbor sites, and many other selected essential elements of information. Working under the most adverse conditions of weather and terrain, and at times so deep in enemy territory that they could not be supported by friendly artillery, the battalion's patrols repeatedly distinguished themselves in displaying a selfless dedication to duty, bold initiative, resourcefulness, and an aggressive fighting spirit. While carrying out the primary mission of the battalion as the "eyes of the division," these patrols additionally accounted for 2,683 confirmed kills and 4,019 probable kills. By their outstanding professional skill, unswerving devotion to duty and uncommon valor, the officers and men of the First Reconnaissance Battalion (Reinforced) upheld the highest traditions of the Marine Corps and the United States Naval Service.

All personnel attached to and serving with the First Reconnaissance Battalion (Reinforced) during the above period, or any part thereof, are hereby authorized to wear the NAVY UNIT COMMENDATION Ribbon.

John H Chafee

Secretary of the Navy

DEPARTMENT OF THE NAVY
HEADQUARTERS UNITED STATES MARINE CORPS
WASHINGTON, D C. 20380

IN REPLY REFER TO

The Secretary of the Navy takes pleasure in presenting the MERITORIOUS UNIT COMMENDATION to

THIRD AMPHIBIAN TRACTOR BATTALION
FIRST MARINE DIVISION (REINFORCED)

for service as set forth in the following

CITATION:

For meritorious service in the Republic of Vietnam from 16 September 1967 to 1 September 1968. At this time the Battalion supported the First Marine Division the 196th and 198th Light Infantry Brigades and the Second Korean Marine Brigade While in direct support, elements of the Battalion participated in 29 named operations which included DRAGONFIRE, MAMELUKE THRUST and ALLENBROOK. This participation consisted of convoy escort, search and destroy, reaction force, resupply, blocking force and medical evacuation missions and many County Fairs The Battalion also actively aided in land clearing operations during construction of the Danang barrier. In addition the Battalion relocated during this period and established a new precedent for the First Marine Division, as it was the first time that a supporting unit was assigned an Area of Responsibility tasked to provide such type security The AOR assigned was one of the most strategic in the Danang area in that it included four mountains, which are the prominent terrain features in east Danang, the strategic U. S. Naval Transmitter site, and four villages with a total population of 5,000 Vietnamese. To meet the security requirements within the AOR, the men of the Battalion had to far exceed the tasks normally assigned to a support unit. The personnel performed the normal support mission during the day and provided security for the Marble Mountain vital area complex at night through active combat patrols in contact with the enemy. Three enemy offensives in the Danang area were triggered in and just adjacent to the Battalion's AOR. By their effective teamwork, aggressive fighting spirit and individual acts of heroism and daring, the men of the Third Amphibian Tractor Battalion successfully repelled the enemy offensives and prevented them from firing mortars or rockets from their AOR onto the Danang vital area or airfield. Although not normally assigned to performing as infantry, the men of this Battalion accounted for themselves in an exceptional manner and exemplified the qualities of courage and skill which were in keeping with the highest traditons of the Marine Corps and the United States Naval Service

DEPARTMENT OF THE NAVY
HEADQUARTERS UNITED STATES MARINE CORPS
WASHINGTON, D. C. 20380

IN REPLY REFER TO

All personnel attached to and serving with the following units of the Third Amphibian Tractor Battalion during the period 16 September 1967 to 1 September 1968, or any part thereof, are hereby authorized to wear the MERITORIOUS UNIT COMMENDATION Ribbon.

    Headquarters and Service Company
    Company A
    Company B

    SUPPORTING UNITS

    Detachment of Company B, 1st Amphibian Tractor Battalion
    1st Platoon, Company B, 5th Amphibian Tractor Battalion
    Detachment of Sentry Dog Platoon, 3d Military Police Battalion
    Detachment of 1st Shore Party Battalion

                    For the Secretary of the Navy,

                    Commandant of the Marine Corps

Glossary

ammo	Ammunition.
Amtracs	Amphibious Tractors, used to transport troops and supplies. Also called LVTs, AmTracs, Tracs, "Hawgs," Amtrac Battalion or AMTRACS.
ARVN	Army of the Republic of (South) Vietnam. A soldier is usually called an "Arvin."
bird	Any aircraft, but usually referring to helicopters.
bunker	Protected area, usually a reinforced hole or dwelling.
CG	Commanding General.
CH-46	(H-46) Boeing Vertol Sea Knight, a twin-turbine, tandem-rotor transport helicopter, designed to carry a four-man crew and seventeen combat-loaded troops.
CH-53	(H-53) Sikorsky Sea Stallion, a single-rotor, heavy transport helicopter powered by two shaft-turbine engines with an average payload of 12,800 pounds. Carries a crew of three and thirty-eight combat-loaded troops.
Charlie	Viet Cong or North Vietnamese, the enemy.
chopper	Helicopter, 'copter, bird.
claymore	Anti-personnel mine.
CO	Commanding Officer.
COC	Combat Operation Center.
county fair	A cordon and search operation in a particular hamlet or village by South Vietnamese troops, police, local officials, and US Marines in an attempt to screen out and register local inhabitants.
CP	Command Post, a tactical headquarters.
C-rations	Combat ration, a gourmet meal of World War II vintage.

di di (Dee Dee) Vietnamese word for "Move out."

DMZ Demilitarized Zone created by the Geneva Accords of 1954 along the 17th parallel dividing South and North Vietnam.

echo Letter E of the phonetic alphabet. Company E or Echo Company.

G-2 Military Intelligence Section. Also, an individual's brain power: "He hasn't got any G-2."

G-3 Military Operations Section.

grunt Marine rifleman or Army infantryman.

gung-ho Introduced as a training slogan for the Marine Second Raider Battalion in 1942 by Colonel Evans F. Carlson, from an abbreviated Chinese word translated as "work together." Zealous.

H&S Company Headquarters and Service Company, sometimes referred to as "Heat and Steam." Composed of administrative clerks, supply clerks, cooks, motor transport, mechanics, radio operators, others. Also, the LVTEs in an Amtrac Battalion.

head Marine and Navy term for a toilet or lavatory. Equates to an Army latrine.

head detail Individuals assigned to clean up head area.

Heat and Steam Headquarters and Service Company.

Huey Popular name for UH-1 series of helicopters.

ID Identification, identification card, identification tag.

KIA Killed in Action.

LVT Landing Vehicle, Tracked. Amphibious Tractor.

LVTE Landing Vehicle, Tracked, Engineer; a lightly armored amphibian vehicle designed for minefield and obstacle clearance. Amtrac, Trac, Hawg.

LVTP Landing Vehicle, Tracked, Personnel; an amphibian vehicle used to land and/or transport personnel.

LZ	Landing Zone.
M-16	American military rifle. Issued to American troops in Vietnam after 1966.
MACV	Military Assistance Command, Vietnam.
MAG	Marine Aircraft Group.
Medevac	Medical evacuation.
MG	Machine gun.
MSR	Main supply route.
NCO	Noncommissioned Officer.
NCOIC	Noncommissioned Officer in Charge.
NSA	Naval Support Activity (i.e., Navy hospital).
nui	Vietnamese word for hill or mountain.
NVA	North Vietnamese Army.
OP	Observation Post.
R&R	Rest and Recreation, Rest and Relaxation.
Reaction Squad	Reserve squad of Marines ready for action when needed. Not always riflemen; however, ready for combat as riflemen, infantrymen, grunts.
Recon	Reconnaissance company or battalion, also patrols or reconnaissance missions. Recon Marines.
reconnaissance	To scout or search for enemy activity. To recon.
Rocker	First lower stripe of enlisted rank insignia formed in a curve, a "rocker." From Staff Sergeant to Sergeant Major rank insignia.
RSM	Regimental Sergeant Major.
RVN	Republic of (South) Vietnam.
sapper	A soldier usually armed with explosives, expert at penetrating defenses.
scuba	Self Contained Underwater Breathing Apparatus (SCUBA).
shrapnel	Metal fragments from an exploding bomb or grenade.
skipper	Commanding Officer of a Company, usually a Captain, sometimes called "Skipper."
SRB	Service Record Book.

Staff NCO   Enlisted Marines with the rank of Staff Sergeant to Sergeant Major. A distinct and select group of NCOs, which have been in continuous existence since a law of 1798 authorized the Commandant of the Marine Corps to appoint a staff of senior enlisted Marines.

TAOR   Tactical Area of Responsibility.

Tet   Vietnamese New Year.

Tet Offensive   Country-wide offensive in early 1968 by Viet Cong and North Vietnamese Army.

Torii   A form of Japanese decorative gateway or portal, consisting of two upright wooden posts connected at the top by two horizontal crosspieces, commonly found at the entrance to Shinto temples.

Tracrat   LVT Marines, crewmen, amtrackers.

USMC   US Marine Corps.

USN   US Navy.

VC   Viet Cong, a term used to refer to the communist guerrilla in South Vietnam; a derogatory contraction of the Vietnamese phrase meaning "Vietnamese Communists."

WIA   Wounded in Action.

wingwiper   Aviation Marine.

XO   Executive Officer, the second in command of a military unit.